AF226236

ABOUT THE AUTHOR

Venuste Nshimiyimana is a Rwandan-born British broadcaster with more than 30 years of experience in international broadcasting. He previously served as TV editor at the BBC in London, where he spent 20 years in various management and editorial positions.

Venuste is the author of *Prélude du Génocide Rwandais*, which looks at the factors that triggered the 1994 genocide of the Tutsis and the massacre of moderate Hutus. He currently works for the Washington-based VOA—Voice of America.

CANDID INTENT

CANDID INTENT

AN ODYSSEY FROM THE BEEB TO BAGHDAD

VENUSTE NSHIMIYIMANA

HAIKONIC BOOKS

—•—

Copyright © Venuste Nshimiyimana, 2023.
The moral right of the author has been asserted.

—•—

First published in the United Kingdom
by Haikonic Books, an imprint of
Haikonic, Ltd.
167-169 Great Portland Street, Fifth Floor
London, WIW 5PF - United Kingdom
www.haikonicbooks.com

—•—

A CIP catalogue record for this book
is available from the British Library
ISBN 978-1-8384712-4-8

—•—

Jacket front image by Farhan Jimale
Additional war concept illustration © Zerfeli
Layout & cover design © *The Point & Pixell Studio*

For my daughters,
Isaro and Astrida.

Men falter at your approaching foot-
steps. Tortured dirges scream on your
lyre of despair. Like a fiery Salamander
you poison the land: growling over
the earth like thunder, vegetation collapsing before you, blood gushing
down mountainsides. Spirit of hatred,
greed, and vengeance!

—ENHEDUANNA
Lament To The Spirit of War

CONTENTS

WHY CANDID INTENT

If you are the impatient type, more interested in books than how they've come to be, you'd be well served to skip this note altogether. For you, the *Introduction* might be a best place to start. However, if you are like me, intrigued by the backstories of paperbacks, wondering about what typeface has been used to achieve the layout, slightly annoyed by having to guess the logic behind a book's title, then you've started right where you should. Please, read on.

WE STARED DOWN at each other. Separated by a dozen miles and a night-time of rolling London neighbourhoods. But we were kept together by the intermediation of *screen* and *ether*. And thus, we were engaged in one of the many late-night *Zoom* calls that went into the prep-work for this book: "A good memoir," my editor said, as he stared back at me down the camera, "just like good wine, is the gift of time. Without time, wine is only unfermented grape juice. And without time, a memoir is a banal collection of news items and anecdotes."

We had been discussing self-censorship. I had the idea that some things about certain people and places must be kept out of the book. If only to avoid litigation, as the result of someone taking offence. My editor, however, felt differently. He believed good memoirs don't bow to *characters* who'd rather not feature in them.

I liked his *good-wine* metaphor, but I needed to get back to writing. A workable understanding of what he meant was crucial.

"Talk to me like I'm four," I said. "It's late and I'm losing focus. What are you saying, exactly?"

"I'm saying that time may blunt your memories, but a memoir is just that—an account of the surviving impressions of past events in your life. So, are you going to write a *memoir* or not?"

Of course, there was no dilemma here. But I'd rather listen for some more.

"You tell me," I said. "Shall I throw in the towel?"

There was a chuckle. "No, you are going to write a *memoir*. And for a start, I propose that you lay to rest your desire for self-censorship. Then, forget about making *this* yet another history book on the Iraq War."

That last bit intrigued me.

"But it's a book about the war," I protested.

"And that's my concern," my editor retorted. And piercing the screen with that analytical stare, and marking his words with the gesture of a lifted finger, he made a point that reshuffled the project as initially conceived. "Apart from what's tied directly to you in a way that's *non-transferable*, there's nothing new or interesting left for a book about Bush's invasion of Iraq. Make this a book that will read like one *unique* masterclass on your life as a broadcaster; one that only you, not even Bob Woodward, could supply."

Bob Woodward? That tickled me a bit. The fellow could speak to all the *Deep Throats* of the world. What could I supply that he couldn't?

I merely intended the question as a gentle tease. But my nightly companion took it seriously. He locked eyes with the screen and took me for a gentle admonishment, while keeping on a twisted smile all the way. "Bob Woodward is not a black man," he stated. "He is not from Rwanda. He speaks no Swahili, no Kinyarwanda, no French. And as far as I know, he has yet to work for the British Broadcasting Corporation. His voice—unlike yours—is not familiar to over 35 million people across the African continent. Your perspective on the world is not that of Woodward or anyone else for that matter. Bob can write anything, but your story."

That made me feel heavy with a weird kind of

emotion. I said, laughing: "You have a way of making me feel bigger than I care to think I am. I owe you a drink."

"Maybe," my editor snapped dismissively. He was willing to stay on track: "One more obvious thing now is that your working title *doesn't work* anymore. What do you think?"

The Palestine Hotel. That was the initial title of the book. Right there, I agreed that the shift of focus just made it redundant. And right there, we decided to drop it. Moments later, we broke away from our umpteenth *Zoom* session, brainstorming for a new title. And we wouldn't have our ultimate *Eureka* moment until several weeks later.

Candid Intent.

Candid, as in *truthful*. *Intent*, as in *purpose*. This ultimate title came out of nowhere. It was the offspring of yet-another *Zoom* session, where my editor relentlessly pressed me to clarify, why the hell, I was writing the book: Was it out of malice? Was it to settle some scores or to set some record straight? Why this memoir?

"We made that clear," I reminded him: "My loyalty now lies with the story—I am writing candidly, from the heart. You may call this, *Operation Candid Intent*."

A couple of days later, I received a gushing text.

"I think we have a title," it read. "*Candid Intent.* Just perfect. Tell me you like it." I was instantly sold on the simplicity of it. And straight away, I said yes.

A QUICK NOTE on style and substance. This memoir is more *fly-on-the-wall* than anything else. It draws primarily from my direct observations, my reporting, my insights—my life. Rather than supply you with a stale record of History, my goal is to connect you with a personal story, conveyed in an intimate voice that places a stock in flow and rhythm.

Out of a deliberate choice, I don't trouble you with tons of distractive footnotes. And to guarantee accuracy in the historical accounts of generally accepted facts, I consulted bibliographical and online resources. They are referenced at the end.

Dialogues are not *verbatim*. They are *reconstructed* to reflect the substantive *truthfulness* of actual conversations and interactions, as best as I remember them.

Now, a point of typography. I use the *italic mode*, on top of any normal usages, to convey emphasis, to indicate quotes that are not *verbatim*, to highlight flashbacks, thoughts, and inner dialogues. And where the real name of a person has been substituted—say, a *Tom* in the real-world is referred to in the book as *Harry*—I subtly draw the reader's attention to the substitution by the use of *italics*.

And finally, the font used to achieve this clean and elegant interior layout is *Sabon*, a serif typeface designed in 1967 by Jan Tschichold for Stempel. It was released by Linotype in 1971. *Sabon* is based on the typefaces of Claude Garamond. It is contemporary, was purposely designed for phototypesetting, and delivers a classic and rounded feel. Please, note that it may have been swapped if you are accessing this as an eBook through a reader like *Kindle*.

And now, with a sense of gratitude, I present you *Candid Intent*.

Enjoy.

WHEN NO ONE IS WATCHING

The Spring of 2003 arrived at last, slowly awaking Mother Nature from its wintry slumber. And that was pleasant to behold. But spring had come along with the disheartening clunk of war. Thousands of miles away from my busy desk in London; this far away in the Arabian Gulf, the scene had been set for the invasion of Iraq, with the United States and Great Britain in the lead role. Along with a supporting cast—a handful of junior partners—they formed what would go down in History as the Coalition.

Now, let's back up a little if you will.

The Year 2001 was for the US an *annus horribilis*. But 2001 was worse still for one *other* country. And that is Afghanistan: To the Mullahs in Kabul, *Judgment*

Day prematurely came about in 2001. And it was rather an earthly affair—not the stuff of an afterlife.

Arguably, the Mullahs had it coming. Defiantly providing a haven for Ben Laden—the unrepentant mastermind of the 9/11 Attacks—was pretty unwise. And as one may remember, in the wake of the attacks, America was a wounded beast. And rightly so. It stomped with mighty fury, and with an acute thirst for vengeance.

For reasons that were obvious, President George W. Bush turned his attention to Afghanistan. Against the Mullahs, Bush had an indisputable case for war. And hasty plans were being thrown together to bring retaliation to the Taliban. However—as though Bush needed a further *casus belli*—he perfunctorily gave the Taliban a last chance of sorts. He asked them to hand over their cumbersome guest.

Quite recklessly, the Taliban told America to get lost. Osama ben Laden—they argued—was a Muslim. And they couldn't possibly hand over a *brother* to the *Great Infidel*. So, they said no. And they were very impolite about it. For that, they were to pay a highest price.

In just a matter of twenty weeks after the attacks, US-led coalition bombs started to rain down on cities across Afghanistan. Within a relative short spell, Muhammad Omar, the chief Mullah—along with his counsels and al Qaeda's fighters—were sent running for cover in the high Afghan mountains. And when the bombing ceased at Tora Bora and Ben Laden was nowhere to be found, the Americans were left foaming at the mouth with frustration.

As it appeared, the war—contrary to the hopes of Donald Rumsfeld, the Secretary of Defence—was not to last just a mere two to six weeks. Why would America fall back home while Ben Laden was still out there, guaranteed to be taunting Uncle Sam very soon in his next video release to Al Jazeera?

Clearly, this business of war was just getting started. And with the rubble of the *Twin Towers* still hot underneath; with the world still stunned by what happened on that horrific day, America—not that it really needed it—could count on a global capital of sympathy. But then, something quite extraordinary happened.

By some sleight of hand, the Bush Administration slowly looked away from Afghanistan, and away from its next-door neighbour, Pakistan, where Ben Laden would be killed a decade later. Bush and his *Pentagon* advisers rather chose to set their sight on Iraq, more than 2,000 kilometres away, across the vast swathes of the Iranian territory.

To be clear, Iraq was one country of a kind, if only because of the nasty tantrums of its surly dictator, Saddam Hussein, notorious for his propensity for *gassing* opposition strongholds. That, however, barely qualified as evidence that Saddam Hussein and Ben Laden were bedfellows who must have teamed up to pull off the 9/11 Attacks. But did evidence really matter?

Obviously, not.

Since the last *Gulf War* in 1991 under Bush's father, America had been in a permanent state of undeclared war with Saddam, the reason why the Clinton Administration worked with Congress to ultimately pass the *Iraq Liberation Act, 1998*. The attacks on 9/11 had just given George Bush a stronger—if a flawed—case for Saddam's removal. And Bush would display a narrow-mindedness in getting what he wanted.

FROM THE SOUTHEAST Wing of Bush House, the London headquarters of the *BBC World Service*, we watched from our computer terminals as all the incredible details of the drama of war unfolded, drifting into the six wings of the building via the internal traffic channels, kept abuzz around the clock by the BBC's extensive network of correspondents and stringers posted in every major city in the world. And this is what we knew for sure: Diplomacy had failed. The heat was peaking up. And violence was now inevitable.

This close to the looming conflagration, no day went by without George Bush issuing one of those hawkish statements, promising regret and sorrow to Saddam. And by now, General Tommy Franks—Head of the US Central Command in the Middle East and beyond—was in the last stage of moving men and logistics to the wider theatre of operations. In fact, at this point, had it not been for that meddlesome fellow, *Monsieur* Jacques Chirac who sat at the Elysée Palace across the Channel, leading the global political opposition to the war, Bush and Blair would have already unleashed fire into the fearful nights of Iraqi cities, where ordinary folks now waited in nail-biting anticipation for death and destruction.

For us at the British Broadcasting Corporation, the upcoming invasion was a kind of a *one-time* equivalent of the Olympics. That was because every event of any significance, let alone this unprecedented war, was a big deal for the BBC. With its *World Service* located in the Strand, the BBC, as we shall discuss, was the perfect *broadcasting equivalent of the United Nations*. The upcoming war—arriving in time to feature in the organisation's records before its hundredth anniversary—was even more significant in one particular regard. Not since the Second World War, had Great Britain been in such a position of having to commit servicemen and logistics to a war zone at such a major scale. Iraq was to be as much a British affair as it was American. It was so much so that America's *Operation Iraqi Freedom* was given its separate British code name—*Operation Telic*.

As it were, while army generals on both sides of the Atlantic put finishing touches to their plans of attack, editorial bosses across the BBC frantically discussed their own strategies. And as the war rhetoric gathered pace and we feverishly shuttled from one editorial briefing to another, it soon became clear that I was being discussed as key asset for the team that the *BBC World Service* would be deploying to the Middle East.

It was a privilege.

However, when the email confirming my deployment arrived at my terminal, it landed an unexpected punch in my gut. *War; large-scale violence; possible massacre and maiming of innocents; chaos and mayhem*—the prospect of that stirred up in me sediments of barely buried memories, setting off mental flashes of a *déjà-vu*.

1994. KIGALI, RWANDA. I was in my late twenties. And life was rather treating me well. Very well, in fact. Four years of higher studies, and a string of assignments here and there in Belgium and Rwanda had given me my credentials of fitness for *trading* in the print and broadcast and communication industries. A brief stint with the Organisation of the African Unity later, the UN came with a job offer. Yes, the *United Nations*—that body born in the wake of the *Second World War*. I mean, I was exceedingly impressed.

Upon my appointment with the UN, I was on cloud nine with elation at my incredible, good fortunes. Temporarily turning my back to broadcasting, I shifted gears; I became a junior information officer at the local headquarters of the international organisation. Such a job would be a big deal anywhere for anyone at such an early stage of their career. It was even more so in Kigali. But fate often had a way of playing nasty tricks on us.

While fate, visiting hopeful prospects upon me, appeared to have given all to me with one generous hand, it wickedly, with the other hand, took everything away, as it set the land of my folks on the rattling tracks to *war, large-scale violence, massacre and maiming of innocents, chaos, and mayhem—the Genocide.*

There was an array of causes to the inter-ethic animosity that had been smouldering across Rwanda. But that is beyond the scope of this introduction. Suffice it to say that our descent into the pit of *Hades* resulted from a nasty long slow burn. Gradually, neighbours, friends, in-laws, colleagues, fellow worshippers, football teammates—out of a deadly sentiment against Tutsis and moderate Hutus—lost their senses, and turned to stocking machetes and clubs and bows and arrows. Next, they would use those blunt weapons in a bloody butchery that would leave an abiding scar on the conscience of Humanity.

In the now-infamous *100 Days of Terror*, the paradisiacal rolling green hills of the Rwandan countryside lost their idyllic allure. Cities, previously awash with God-fearing fervour, turned into deathly haunts for monsters in human shapes. In the stretch of urban yards and blocks, no refuge was there for hundreds of thousands of souls, whose desperate attempts at running away from tragedy were nothing but extended agonies.

As the nation spun on itself in the turmoil of unrestrained madness, options thinned out severely for those who were at the receiving end of the bloodshed. Getting killed became more of a certainty.

And the best of hopes was to get the hell out. But how to get the hell out when a dash in any direction was to potentially deliver oneself into the trap of a rabid killer lying in ambush, hugging a machete close to their murderous chest?

No, amid the torpors of the massacre, there was no unscathed ones—not even those who ultimately managed, at the cost of extreme hardship, to escape through the wilderness of Northern and Southern Zaïre, or by way of exfiltration in highly protected corteges of foreign forces.

As a UN employee, I was exfiltrated. And I could attest that surviving was just the beginning of long years of residual anguish and pain. The atrocities we witnessed irretrievably claimed something deeply intimate in each of us. If anything, that haunting survivor's remorse would morph into a heavy slab of a burden to bear. I can say that. Because I know it for sure.

THE SEEDS OF human follies, the type which turns a kind heart into a hardened rock that is impervious to the suffering of children and of women, and of the elderly; such seeds are sown in darkness. They often sprout to yield nothing but fruits of large-scale atrocities when no one is watching. If journalism, my trade, is about anything at all, it is that it should shine a spotlight on such places where darkness comes to gather, and where men, driven by hatred or by greed or by both, would stop at nothing to sow and to water the grim seeds of death and destruction.

In that fateful April of 1994 in my beloved Rwanda, the spotlight arrived very late; the world had been looking elsewhere when the blood-fest took hold of one neighbour after another. You do not need to have stood in my shoes back then to understand how I have come to hold this as self-evident: that—collectively, as Humanity—we have a duty never to aid and abet murders and massacres by looking away when the storm of war and strife is gathering.

To understand this view of mine is to understand why I agreed to my deployment in Baghdad during the war. When my BBC bosses reached their decision to despatch me to the Middle East, I reached deep inside myself to repress the dreadful memories of our *100 Days of Terror*. Quite simply, I had to show up for duty. Because darkness strives where the lights are out. I wanted to play a part in shedding the light in Iraq, where civilians—through no fault of their own— stood in harm's way.

Of course, upon accepting the assignment, I tacitly surrendered myself to the possibility that I might not return alive. With such uncertainty hanging over my head, the idea of a book at the time would have qualified as one of those proverbial cases of *building castles in Spain*. But then, I survived and went home safe to my family.

In the intervening years, I would be haunted by a sense of unfinished business whenever the issue of the War found its way back into a conversation, of which I was a party. And some of the questions I would field came to be much predictable: What was it like to be looking out for headlines amid the noise of falling bombs and the wailing of the bereaved? How much recklessness does it take for anyone to risk life and limb for playing messenger amid the mayhem of war? And what difference does it make to shine the spotlight on a war that was being blatantly fought on a lie and in defiance of decency and truth?

Debating these questions gradually became more than merely academic. They turned into a recurrent exercise in introspection; one that forced the journalist in me to face myself in a candid assessment of our assumed influence as men of the media. Yeah, we are part of the *Fourth Estate*. But what power have we got left when the rules known to civilised society are overridden and suddenly no longer apply?

All that said—and as aforementioned—the origins of this book are not to be found in my experience grappling with these sobering questions. It took the relentless prodding of my editor for the idea of the project to coalesce, as the 20th anniversary of the war drew closer.

Now, what is it that I have to tell you?

Well, we now have the final word on Bush and Blair's transgression against the Iraqi people; we now know the scale of the devastation they had left behind—most about the dead and where they are buried is common knowledge. So, this is not a *wide-shot* account of the Coalition's invasion of Iraq. It's my *soul-level* account of it. And my hope is to properly address—with hindsight and at a long last—those old stubborn questions, through the subjective lens of what had been a slice of my life as a broadcaster with one of the world leading news organisations.

In tying up the loose ends, I won't restrain from offering you an intimate glimpse into what goes in the making of a global news story, and how top professionals go about reporting it, grappling with their own values, their own hopes, their own insecurities. At any rate, I will have achieved my goal upon handing copies of this book to my dear daughters, Isaro and Astrida. This memoir of their father is a slice of a greater story—the story of their family. But I dimly entertain a subsidiary hope.

Perhaps, many years from now, students tasked with studying the war or the *BBC World Service* may stumble upon some format of this book at the British Library, or the Library of Congress. On reading it, if they come across a detail or a point of perspective, which they would not have found anywhere else, that would be a formidable bonus. And from whichever dimension I might be residing then, if I could peer through and see satisfaction etched on a face, I would certainly give off a wink of contentment.

CHRONOLOGY

1990—1991	Iraq's invasion of Kuwait prompts US-led Gulf War that ends in Saddam's defeat on 28th February 1991
3 Apr 1991	In the wake of Kuwait's invasion, UN creates UNSCOM to oversee disarmament operations in Iraq
Jun 1991—Feb 1997	UNSCOM inspectors detect and destroy WMDs and related facilities
21 Jun 1997	Iraq restricts access to certain sites; later orders out inspectors of US nationality

31 Oct 1998	Clinton signs *Iraq Liberation Act* into law, pledging support to Saddam's Opposition for his removal
16 Dec 1998	UNSCOM withdraws from Iraq
16—19 Dec 1998	Clinton orders strikes on Iraqi targets in what was code-named *Operation Desert Fox*
17 Dec 1999	UNSCOM disbanded and replaced by UNMOVIC amid allegations of CIA infiltration
20 Jan 2001	George W. Bush becomes 43rd US president
11 Sept 2001	Attacks on Twin Towers and the Pentagon
20 Sept 2001	Taliban given ultimatum to hand over Osama Ben Laden or face war

25 Sept 2001	Defence Secretary Donald Rumsfeld spells out *Operation Enduring Freedom*, aka *War on Terror*
7 Oct 2001	US-led coalition begins air-strikes in Afghanistan
13 Nov 2001	US-backed *Northern Alliances* enter Kabul as Taliban flee in disarray for mountains
6—17 Dec 2001	The Battle of Tora Bora
29 Jan 2002	In State of Union Address, President Bush names Iraq as part of an Axis of Evil
5—7 Apr 2002	Blair and Bush discuss Iraq at Crawford Ranch secret meeting
12 Sept 2002	Bush tells UN that Saddam produces WMDs and sponsors terrorism

24 Sep 2002	Blair tells Parliament that intel on Saddam's WMDs is extensive, detailed, and authoritative
8 Nov 2002	UN Security Council adopts *Resolution 1441*
27 Nov 2002	UN inspection of Saddam's alleged WMD programmes resumes
7 Dec 2002	Saddam submits declaration of weapon programmes to UN inspectors
5 Feb 2003	Secretary of State Colin Powell makes dramatic case for war at the UN
14 Feb 2003	France's Foreign Minister de Villepin delivers speech at UN opposing eventual war in Iraq
15 Feb 2003	Day of coordinated protests in 600+ cities across the world as war looms

26 Feb 2003	Bush in remarks at Hilton Hotel in DC says threat by Saddam must be confronted
18 Mar 2003	Bush's 48-hours ultimatum orders Saddam out of Iraq. Meanwhile, UN inspectors leave country
20 Mar 2003	War begins with the bombing of a bunker in Baghdad followed by sustained airstrikes
8 Apr 2003	US army tank unleashes round into *The Palestine Hotel*, fatally wounding three media personnel
9 Apr 2003	US soldiers take control of Baghdad after capture of city airport five days earlier
10—13 Apr 2003	Respective falls of Kirkuk, Mosul, and Saddam's hometown of Tikrit
1 May 2003	President Bush declares end to major combats

25 May 2003	Paul Bremer, US *de facto* Head of State of Iraq, disbands Saddam's armed forces
May 2003—2008	Iraq descends into violent insurgency and then sectarian civil war
19 Sept 2003	Suicide attack on UN HQ in Baghdad kills 23, including top UN official Vieira de Mello
13 Dec 2003	Capture of Saddam, executed three years later for war crimes and crimes against humanity
24 Jan 2004	WMD search ends with official admission that "we were almost all wrong"
28 Apr 2004	Evidence of prisoner abuse inside the US-run Abu Ghraib prison becomes public

14 Jul 2004	*Butler Review* finds that intelligence justifying the war was "unreliable"
4 Nov 2008	Senator Obama elected President with pledge to withdraw US troops from Iraq
30 Aug 2010	Obama announces end of combat operations in Iraq
15 Mar 2011	Start of the 11-year civil war in Syria marked by unprecedented refugee crisis
19 Mar 2011	NATO-led intervention in Libya triggers on-going Sahel terrorism crisis
2 May 2011	Osama bin Laden killed in Abbottabad, Pakistan
18 Dec 2011	Last US soldiers leave Iraq, ending a nearly nine-year military mission

2011—2013	Fresh Sunni insurgency against Shiite-led government
Dec 2013—Dec 2017	The Islamic State Insurgency in Iraq and Syria
10 June 2014	Mosul captured by Islamic State, major event in take-over by IS of Northern Iraq
6 Jul 2016	*Chilcot Inquiry* finds UK joined Iraq invasion before peaceful options had been exhausted
15 Aug 2021	Taliban recaptures Kabul after US withdraws forces

THE METHOD IN THE MADNESS

Shortly before we drove across the city gate, I was struck by a glaring irony. Spelled out in Arabic and English, a road sign did its best in extending a promise of hospitality to us. WELCOME TO BAGHDAD, the sign proclaimed.

Sadly, the congenial message failed to elicit in me the predictable excitement I normally experienced upon crossing the boundaries of any new city. Rather than excitement, it set my pulse running a little faster.

Welcome? I thought. *But welcome to what? To our possible death?*

To be honest, I wasn't sure what I wanted the road sign to say. Perhaps, I was surprised instinctually that it was there at all; that it was not torn down by some *Fedayeen* fighter, hopelessly intent on not marking up the limits of Baghdad for easy identification by the invading armies.

When we pulled up at last in front of *The Palestine Hotel*, I was taken aback to be welcomed by the same effusive message of hospitality, this time on the part of *actual* residents of the city, who had to lie low as the *Warthog* fighter jets flew around dropping bombs.

"*Ahlan wa sahlan*," they chanted.

That's Arabic for *Welcome*.

Again, I wondered, "*Welcome to what?*"

I would soon discover there was method to this madness. The arrival into Baghdad of *free-willing* outsiders, with no business to do with the invading armies, was taken for something of a solidarity. Moreover, we represented a promise of employment for people who so badly wanted to work.

As it happened, we had unwittingly brought false hope into this place where *Doomsday* seemed to have arrived much ahead of those scriptural End Times.

PART I

This benign Tower of Babel, the scene
of so many great broadcasting moments,
and the home of so many broadcasters
over the years.

—MARK THOMPSON
Former BBC Director-General

Chapter 1

NATION SHALL SPEAK UNTO NATION

The day after the fall of Baghdad, it was another morning in the life of the iconic *Bush House* building in Central London. As I made my way from Charing Cross down the busy Strand pavements and approached those marble steps that led through the portico into the Bush House lobby, I felt a familiar awe washing over me, which provisionally untethered me from my silent rehearsals for the crucial meeting that awaited beyond the dramatic facade of the complex.

Oh, yeah—there was an imperceptible sense of mysticism about this place; one that I had hoped to ultimately become unimpressed about; but one which I never came around to claiming as a definite conquest. And you may wonder why. Well, some legends are sacred with no need for surrounding taboos. And Bush

House was one of those sacred legends. And that was enough to tell anyone that Bush House was not just a brick-and-mortar complex: Nowhere else did the BBC motto—*Nation Shall Speak Unto Nation*—assume as much a literal meaning as here.

But my point is, Bush House was an organism with a life of its own. And Bush House lived unapologetically.

The iconic building stands on a special traffic island in The Strand, at the heart of the old London quarter of Aldwych. There, it seems to have been backed and boxed into position by the busy Kingsway, a street that morphs into an underpass and into a left turn, ending right where Bush House begins.

And as though the complex, with its Centre Block flanked by a cluster of six wings, might someday grow tired of the eternal din of traffic and decide to spring to life and run off into the farthest reaches of the London skyline, Bush House is discretely guarded on all sides.

It is guarded to the east, by the Royal Courts of Justice, right at the threshold of The City; much closer-by to the north, it is guarded by the London School of Economics; and to the south—almost up against the embankment of the Thames River—Bush House is guarded by the antique church of *Saint Mary The Strand* and the even more iconic Somerset House.

Perhaps because of the Iraq War, people often asked me on my BBC duty trips whether the name of the building had anything to do with the Bush family. Having been introduced to the history of Bush House from the inside, I had an accurate answer: No, Bush House had nothing to do with the Texans—the father and son who had managed to come the closest to founding an American presidential dynasty.

All the same, this *quintessentially British building* as the BBC would describe it; this building that's been given a *Grade II* listing by *Historic England* on the account of its architectural importance: this building saw the light of day as the brainchild of an American—one Mr. Irving T. Bush. And it was after this particular *Bush* that the building was named.

Why?

As any rookie joining the BBC at the time would have learned from an induction flyer or at a welcome session, Irving was an industrialist scion of old money. In the early 1920s, he created an Anglo-American trading organisation, and wanted a home for it at the heart of London. His plan was for the future *Bush House* to serve as an international trading centre. Irving being a man with the wherewithal to push through his pet project, Bush House would soon be commissioned and constructed under his watchful supervision.

The building would take years to fully come together. And by the time the last wing was added in 1938, Irving's brainchild was hailed as the most expensive building in the world. In fact, an envelope of $10 million had gone into the construction of the trading centre. That was a serious amount of money in the 1930s.

However, cost was in no way the reason why the iconic building would become in later years so familiar to hundreds of millions of people around the world—people who might not even have ever visited the UK.

In 1938, alongside its *Empire Service*, which aired programming in English to White subjects of the Crown in the British colonies and dominions, the BBC introduced its first-ever service in foreign language—*BBC Arabic*. It was a response to Mussolini's use of radio to spread fascist propaganda in the Arab World, where the Italian leadership used the nascent *Palestinian Issue* to whip up anti-British sentiment. *BBC Arabic* would immediately serve as a template for two other language units—*Spanish* and *Portuguese*. And with that, the foundation for the *BBC World Service* was laid, and its portfolio of broadcasts would expand considerably with the outbreak of World War II. Yes, the war marked a turning point for the BBC World Service.

During the period, the organisation would serve as a lifeline for many people living under Nazi or Japanese occupation, providing them with news and information from the outside world, giving them hope that peace would eventually return. The *World Service* came out of World War II as a truly global institution. And ever since, it has played a vital role in shaping the world we live in today.

By the time I joined the organisation in the late nineties, it had been operational for almost 60 years and was now producing programmes in 45 languages.

But where *and how* does *Bush House* come into the picture?

The *Empire and General Overseas Services* were initially based in West London, alongside the BBC domestic radio services. Three years into the war, Broadcasting House was bombed by Nazi Germany. There arose the necessity to mitigate any possible downtime in transmission at such a crucial time. BBC bosses looked one mile eastward across London. There, next to Coven Gardens—the breeding ground of thespian London—they spotted a suitable venue to house some of the language services.

Since Bush House wasn't purposely built for broadcasting, the arrangement was meant to be temporary. And that was mainly why the BBC never had any plan of acquiring the building and never did acquire it.

At any rate, the temporary move turned into a long-term tenancy. By 1958, all the language units relocated to the building, and Bush House's transformation into a *Benign Babel Tower* was complete: The largest global hub of independent news and cultural storytelling was fully operational—The world had its *United Nations* of broadcasting, and at Bush House, *Nation Shall Speak Unto Nation* became more than just a motto.

The BBC, assuming no false modesty, advertised Bush House as the *world reference point* for global conversation. And indeed, if Bush House was not talking about something happening in some corner of the world, it certainly was not worth talking about. Yes, the world came to London to make its voice global.

For *Official Britain*, that wasn't bad. In fact, *Bush House* would earn the rather enviable reputation in Westminster circles as the *Jewel in the BBC's crown*. And that was an intimidating argument; one that was strong enough to convince misguided politicians never to go after the *BBC World Service* the wrong way, as such would result in a perfect case of picking up the wrong fight. We, at Bush House, were talking to the world; the world was listening; and that was power. Politicians knew not to mess with Bush House.

But everything ultimately comes to an end. Bush House, as the *world reference point for global conversation,* ended in 2012. As we prepared, with great nostalgia, to vacate the building for a return westward where the BBC had upgraded its headquarters into what's now known as *New Broadcasting House,* we were proudly reminded of how much—over the years—Bush House had witnessed history in the making.

"The services have broadcast events that have changed and shaped the world," the BBC stated in one piece of internal literature. "De Gaulle's broadcasts to the *Free French*—some originating from Broadcasting House; famous speeches by [Winston] Churchill; Hungary's desperate call for help as Russian tanks rolled into Budapest; the fall of the Berlin Wall; the genocide in Rwanda; the war in Kosovo; and 9/11 are just a few."

Yes. Just a few, indeed. And part of the interminable list of events that had got Bush House abuzz was America's response to the 9/11 attacks, of which the invasion of Iraq was just one prominent episode.

Naturally, this Thursday—the day after the fall of Baghdad on 9 April 2003—on yet another morning in the life of Bush House, this complex on the special traffic island in *The Strand,* geared up to add whole new chapters to a long ongoing story: the story of helping the world make sense of itself.

And this Thursday, as I strode onto the marble steps and soon validated my pass with the *Security Team* and was waved through into the building, I childishly marvelled at the efficiency of the system. I marvelled at how, like clockwork, today would unfold as did yesterday and those countless days before. Yes, the big stories could always change. But the main acts of the daily drama at Bush House remained the same.

First, the ticking clocks would nudge the night shifts along the arc of time. As they come into touch with the rising sun, they would slowly melt away into the ether, down the path to oblivion. On the rooftop—or by the edge of the footbridge to the Southeast Wing— a few rabid smokers would stand there indulging in their guilty pleasure, and would behold as the buildings on this side of the Thames gradually become awash with the morning sun light.

Throughout the recurrent cycle of transitions, Bush

House would only dose up for a brief spell. Then, it would stir up and return to full alertness. By 9:00 a.m., as editors and output producers from the myriad of services gathered for the Central Editorial Meeting, the night would seem distant. Sometimes—depending on the weight of that breaking news—the memory of the night, as consigned in handover notes, would have faded away. And the night would then seem *really* as distant as if it never existed.

THIS THURSDAY MORNING at around 10:30, the night was not yet that distant—certainly not forgotten. The spirit of the night was still hanging over when the spritely woman, who wore her golden hair short in a no-frills fashion, finished a call at her desk in the Centre Block.

Before taking her seat at the editorial table where attendants were already in position, she stepped to the large window of the office, overlooking the courtyard of the complex. There, she tinkered with the venetian blinds, and the soft morning light streamed through. Seamlessly, it blended with the timid neon lights beaming down from the low ceiling.

"Sorry for that," the chirpy, light-stepped woman apologised. No one knew why she was apologising. But it was sure, on her part, one indication of some standing considerateness. Anyway, immediately, as she pivoted around on those light steps, she gathered that everyone had not arrived yet.

"Let's give them five more minutes, shall we?" she suggested, after quickly directing her easy and inquisitive eyes to the GMT clock on the wall, taking note of the time.

The woman—Kari Blackburn—had expected no rebuttal to her gentle suggestion.

And none indeed was put forth.

"It's important that we are all on the same page," Kari clarified as if to win over anyone who might be protesting silently. "Beyond any outstanding editorial point that's there to be made, the BBC's duty of care to you should be clearly articulated for all to understand. So, just five more minutes and we shall get started."

As it turned out, less than one minute longer was what we needed to wait: The two tardy fellows, hurrying down the corridors, obviously must have had their eyes on those peripatetic needles of time. And much sooner than later, they were panting along through the door.

Moments later, we were deeply absorbed in the subject matter of our briefing—the *literally* bloody war in Iraq.

Chapter 2

THE MISSION AND THE ROADMAP

The furry rodent carelessly sniffed its way along the bottom edge of the wall and came under a cross of stares from a dozen pairs of eyes when a voice from around the editorial table reported clearly, "We have an intruder, there!" That was enough of a dangerous alert and should have alarmed the rat. But the critter seemed adamant about asserting some kind of right to its presence here and decided to stay unfazed. A correct call of judgement from this furry *fella*. We were not about to pause the meeting and hunt down the thing. No, we just stared at it and rather found amusement in the rodent's magnanimous hubris as it went on sniffing for a while before calmly retreating out of sight.

The brief production brought to us by the rat

definitively came to a close with a random comment about the *Pest Control guys* and how their handling of the flourishing population of rats at Bush House seemed only to make them fatter and more fearless. At that, the room laughed, and we returned our focus to the matter at hand.

SINCE THIS WAS the latest in a long series of editorial briefings on the war, Kari Blackburn was bound to repeat herself. But that wasn't a chore for the lady. As a quintessential BBC manager, Kari saw virtue in repetition—repetition clarified misunderstandings; it renewed opportunities for challenging sloppy thinking; it reduced the likelihood of blunders and bad decisions: *To repeat* is a simple act of responsibility, but often a very consequential one. Certainly, it allowed a manager to cover their back. Anyway, this is the snapshot of what the Boss had just been repeating:

The team we are sending out is a reinforcement, because the demand on our corps of correspondents in the Middle East is intense. And with so many things happening at a time, we need to have more eyes and ears in Iraq. So far, there has been little said about the impact of this campaign on the Iraqi people. This needs to change.

"Unless the ebb and flow of events come to dictate otherwise, you will be reporting directly to your respective home services," Kari said. "But from a practical point of view, the team will operate as one news-gathering unit, looking after each other, checking and sharing stories, comparing sources. We are *One BBC*—and you are not to be competing against one another. And our overriding rule applies of course."

The overriding rule was an elaborate variant of a well-known mantra of our trade—*If you are getting it first, first get it right*. To BBC editorial bosses, less was stressed on the speed aspect of things: a scoop is worthless if it might end up inaccurate, hopelessly incomplete, or as a total fake. We had to absolutely get that straight. Yes, we were the BBC—the global leader in news: What we got wrong would be a *wrong* of catastrophic proportions. And especially on this war, we'd better be late in *getting it right*, rather than rush and get it all wrong. And that, Kari wanted anyone who might have forgotten to just remember. And for that, she would gladly repeat herself.

At typical BBC editorial meetings, even when there was little to disagree on, there would always be some producer who would seek to interrupt and confound the speaker, sometimes just for the heck of it. Any stranger to newsroom atmosphere might see there an electable ground for grievance. Certainly, some youngsters joining newsrooms today, having been conditioned by social media to easily take offence at uncomfortable interactions, would jump to the conclusion that they are being disrespected and undermined. But that was never the spirit. It was just part of the daily test of being in news, this business of shoving your nose literally in other people's business. No, before you were cleared to do that in the name of the whole newsroom, you ought to be able to defend the merit of your propositions even under the most stressful of circumstances. That was how complacent stories were kept out of running orders. To interrupt without prior curtesies was quite customary.

Today, however, we listened politely, without interruption, as Kari Blackburn pressed ahead with this reminder of editorial fundamentals; things that we all understood well—in fact very well to the point that they amounted to something of a dogma. But uninterrupted as she was, the Boss decided to invite interruption all the same, perhaps out of a suspicion that our patience was more politeness than anything.

"Before we review what we intend to achieve," the senior exec offered, "would you like to tell me: have you substantively discussed your assignment with your families? Are they supportive, apprehensive?"

As far as I was concerned, I desired not to make of my assignment anything else but a *normal* work thing. To treat it as more than *normal* work would border on the dramatic. And instead of reassuring the family, it would produce the opposite effect. So, yes—I told Dedeli, my wife, and the girls about the assignment. But I refused to turn it into a topic for a *substantive* dinner-table discussion. So, I thought that others around the table might have something better to offer that could satisfy the inquiry of our chief. But no one rushed to do such a thing. Instead, colleagues looked at each other in surprise. They were not used to being asked personal questions in editorial meetings.

"Well, that's fine," Kari said, seeing that no answer was forthcoming. "What's important is that, now or later, if you don't feel this is the right assignment for you, I will accept that *it's not the right assignment for you*. You can drop me an email anytime if you wish to talk to me one-on-one. But I am sure you appreciate why you've long been enlisted to be part of this."

"Interesting," someone teased. "Shall we say that we happen to harbour some superpowers we don't know of?"

Kari liked the levity, and it made her chuckle off. "Superpowers!?" she exclaimed. "In fact, you can put it that way. But what I mean is, you are part of this team because you have something unique to bring to our mission: Some of you have experience covering events in hostile environments. And some have a direct connection with the region. Or it may be that you are the only one from your service who sees a development opportunity here and are willing to seize it. But there is one exception, if I may say."

Here, Kari's gaze across the table found me. "Venuste…" she called my name aloud, waving a hand in my direction for those who might want to match the name to a face. Eyes followed the movement of the hand. I became for a moment the centre of attention. "You probably have not been part of the same team with Venuste before," she told the room as she introduced me. "Venuste is from Rwanda. He has been with the BBC for... how many years again?"

"Six years," I said, backing that up with a firm nod.

"Ah, already!?" she exclaimed. "Seems to me just as yesterday when you first brought in your family to visit the studios. Your daughter must now be a lady, Venuste."

For a while, the formidable Kari Blackburn went off at a tangent to tell the room how Isaro, my first born, spoke no word of English when we arrived in Britain; of how Isaro, all the same, went on to be a regular at winning "stars" in her classroom—*stars* for good conduct, for homework regularly well done.

Kari was accurate. I just couldn't remember ever telling her all of that. But it was not surprising: Kari was immediate and recessive in her retention of details we shared with her in response to her gentle expressions of curiosity. This was the extent to which Kari knew the folks on staff under her management. This English woman must have brought back to Britain a great store of African warmth from her Tanzanian stay.

"Venuste has a wonderful gift of languages," the boss now told the room when she had seen her tangent all the way through. She appeared to annoy one or two colleagues. Then again, it didn't take much to bore a journalist: Journalists took issue with any form of personal praise. We are wired to find the fault lines in sentimental deliberations. When we are faced with the sentimental stuff, we wonder about the opposite—the most embarrassing possible truth about the subject under praise.

However, some of us who rise up to become managers quickly discover that the art of successful team management and the default scepticism that journalism requires are rather a bad mix. In other words, managing journalists demands of the manager to be less of a *hard-ass* journalist.

"Venuste speaks four different BBC broadcast languages," Kari elaborated, proceeding somewhat to disclose my claim to *superpower*. "Venuste," she called aloud once more, shifting her focus to me again, "I am rather glad that you've readily agreed to undertake this assignment, long before Bush issued his ultimatum to Saddam. By having you there—as we have already discussed—I am covering not just *BBC French*. As well, I will be covering *BBC Swahili*, *BBC Great Lakes*, *BBC Focus on Africa*, and *Network Africa*."

At this point, eyes converged anew in my direction, as if to check who exactly was this guy that seemed to be so well set that he might never be out of a broadcasting job. Even the couple of serious faces that had appeared to be annoyed by Kari's initial soap-opera about my daughter now stared at me more respectfully, more inquisitively. I knew not what to do of the moment.

See—Before joining the BBC, I never viewed it as anything special that I spoke several languages. Sure,

I have always known that it is harder to be obtuse, to be intolerant, to be viscerally tribal when you speak more than one language: Any additional language that we speak grants us a tenancy into a new cultural universe. At least, that has been my experience. And it rather made it easier for me to embrace difference wherever I encountered it. And that was what I found the most wonderful with speaking more than one language. Gratifying enough, in itself.

But when a manager tells you that it's more than that; that it's some *superpower* and is willing to lavish you with genuine praise over it, it feels so damn good. I often thought that Kari—as much as she did—valued my linguistic assets because she was herself a polyglot. But I never doubted that my universe would have been a lot narrower, had it not been for the joys of multilingualism. What a great bonus to be publicly commended for it!

As I now considered this moment, I found it opportune to remind myself that I should accept the compliment with grace, but without letting it get to my head.

"The boss is being too generous," I told the table. And then this to Kari: "But I love the idea of me as *four reporters rolled into one.*"

"Well, that's what you will be, Venuste," Kari shot back, with insistence. "So, feel free not to be modest. I will have in you *four reporters rolled into one.*" Colleagues nodded, a silent chorus of fair play. "As far as *value for money* goes, it doesn't get any better."

"Thank you, boss," I said, overwhelmed.

Having said enough on my account, the editor decided to move on. And in what was a spoof of one recurrent famous line in the *Mission: Impossible* movies, she announced playfully, "Gentlemen… your mission, should you choose to accept—" The room burst into a laughter as soon as we realised what she was doing there.

Kari gave it up and joined in the merriment. And a moment later, she returned to assuming her business-like demeanour, and gave us what was rather a pretty pep talk. And here it is in substance:

Yeah, the war in Iraq is history in the making. As a BBC, we are a serious news brand. And as we have done since the beginning of the war, we must continue to explain and to report all aspects of this conflict in a manner that's trustworthy and authoritative.

Our mission is to let the world know if the Coalition ever finds these weapons of mass destruction, and it will be a major storyline if it doesn't, as it is likely. We shall shine the spotlight on any violation of human rights.

We shall do all of that while staying safe, while sticking ruthlessly to the BBC's core values of independence, impartiality, trust, and accountability. Let's make ordinary Iraqi people come alive in our reporting.

"If our journalism ever came out of this war any stronger," Kari concluded rather gravely, "it will be down to scrutiny on the part of *non-embeds*. In this war—like any other—where information itself is a weapon, embedded journalism is bound to be fraught with red herrings. "

Kari's concluding remarks were no criticism. It was sagacity. And it reflected the BBC's suspicions towards the separate *embed programmes* of the US and the British Armed Forces.

The obvious problem to contend with was that *independence* and a desire for a *380-degree oversight* on the conflict were likely to get you killed, either as a deliberate target or accidentally in a friendly fire.

As it were, our mission—to stay alive while catching a true full picture of the ongoing war—was a real-life *mission: impossible*. That was why, in the end, the War in Iraq—though having been the most reported-on of all wars ever fought—went down in History as the media's most seriously botched-up job.

Chapter 3

THE MEAN STUFF OF
GOSSIPING LIPS

It might have been the day after our ultimate editorial meeting on the war. Yes, that day. Or a little earlier. But it was certainly after one of the many get-togethers of our ad hoc select team. What I remember for sure is that Kari Blackburn had then stolen me away for a chat over a cup of tea. Not within Bush House. But across the Strand where we sat in a coffee shop during the post-lunch quieter hour.

Before Iraq was brought up, there had first been a banter about inconsequential stuff—perhaps the weather, the London traffic; perhaps the merit of speaking one language as opposed to another. Yes, such stuff. Then, we arrived at the real point on our little agenda.

"How do you *deeply* feel about this duty trip?"

Kari had probed without any more gravity than necessary. On the contrary, her habitual happy gaze felt lighter on me as I met it and held onto it. "Going to a war zone is something unique if you see what I mean. It's fine to have cold feet. Especially, if your family is not onboard with this. I will understand. So, be at liberty and speak to me. Quite openly. There's no one here to judge. What's your heart whispering to you?"

I took time to palm my face in an idle fashion, then complied with Kari's instruction. And freely, I spoke.

"You are giving me an opportunity to break away from the office doldrums, the routine," I said. "But above all, it is truly an honour to have been handpicked by you for this assignment. However, I've got one genuine question for you, Boss."

"Shoot away, my dear."

"How fair can you say that you have been towards any of my teammates who might have relished at the opportunity to undertake this duty trip?"

Kari did a double take, looking suspiciously at me. "Wait, has someone been complaining of unfairness?"

Knowing *BBC French* and the unabated shenanigans of its drama kings and queens, Kari was sure someone must have been running their mouth.

And yeah, they were.

And in a spiteful way.

I confirmed the Boss's hunch with silence and a brief eyeroll.

"Oh, yet again!" the woman exclaimed, as she went

on. "Isn't that lovely and very predictable, Venuste. Now, please, don't hold this back: let me hear how I might have committed that sin of unfairness." She froze her gaze on me, eager to hear me out; eager to understand.

"I won't drop names if you may," I said, shifting a tad in my seat. It was always unwise to drop names unless one was serious about pursuing a formal complaint.

"That's fine," she nodded.

"Great," I said. "But someone, as we can agree, is always complaining at *BBC French*. And here, more than just one, in fact. But I'll just say one colleague who wouldn't volunteer for a reporting duty even in the BBC's backyard at the Royal High Courts is sure that I am being made favours."

"Favours?" Kari forced a smile.

"Well, they go around abusing such big words as *office nepotism*. So, I naturally wonder whether they might have a point. I mean, am I being unduly made favours without my explicit knowledge?" I laughed.

"This might appear serious to you, Venuste," Kari said calmly, wearing a thoughtful air. "But when you have been the best colleague you can be, don't mind the gossip. If you want to rise up to manage your Service one day—as I know you will—be kind. Show understanding to the gossiping lips that may surround you. Stand up to those gossipers by not giving a damn. It's a character-building exercise."

I nodded.

And she took a knowing break and had a good swig at her tea.

"Now, on the issue of my reported unfairness, you must take this from me," Kari resumed upon resettling the cup into place. "There is not a single producer in your team whose idea of a favour right now is to be deployed amid the bloody ruins of Iraq. That aside, managers will sometimes bypass the polite formalities of inviting interests from uninterested people who may never show initiative on their own, or who might plainly be unqualified for certain duties. Sometimes, doing so is more responsible and a better use of our limited time."

"Sometimes," I agreed. "But how about in this case?"

"Oh, my dear! As I said, with your command of four BBC broadcast languages, who the hell in your team can even come close to being more suitable than you for this particular duty trip? Tell me!"

I didn't respond. Because her question sounded rhetorical to me. Plus, I didn't feel comfortable with bragging to the Boss that, indeed, I was the best in the team, and that everyone else was conceivably beneath what I could accomplish. But seeing that I was not about to toot my own horn, the Boss turned her question differently.

"Let's try this," she said: "What objectively do you think might disqualify you for this duty trip, even if there were colleagues willing to compete against you for it?" Turned this way, the question was a lot easier to answer.

"I am a capable big boy," I boasted uneasily, laughing, and enjoying her renewed confidence in me. "I am a big boy, Boss. And there seems to absolutely be nothing about this assignment that's too much for me to handle."

She smiled. "Why don't you tell that to the competition?" I got her drift. She was trying to lighten the mood. Was anything really worth the tension here?

Responding to Kari's desire for light-heartedness, I said with a chuckle, "I would have loved to face some active competition. It would have been more pleasant to piss off the passive-aggressive losers I would have out-classed under your stated criteria." For measure, I laughed open-heartedly. Sometimes, one just had to laugh.

"Well," Kari said, standing up, "I hope then that you are ready for Baghdad. Because you are going to forget the gossiping lips at *BBC French*, and then you are flying out there to do a great job. Now, take the week off if you need to do some more reading about Saddam, if you want to make calls to better understand how Jesus might have told Bush to start this war."

Then Kari made merry out of her own joke. I joined her in laughing, because her quip was funny under the light of what Bush had been saying in those speeches, talking about *axes of evil* and whatnot.

AS THE BOSS and I walked back across the Strand into Bush House, I noted that we had quite rightly avoided bringing up the credible elements of danger that came with my assignment. And that was because it had been fully addressed before.

It would be taken care of by serious people who were paid good money by the BBC; people who knew how to survive a war zone; people who had made an art form out of teaching survival skills to war correspondents.

Chapter 4

THE ROAD TO BOOTCAMP

At the window seat of the *National Express* coach to Berkshire, I drank cheap tea as I reviewed printouts of emails from the lady who had been flooding us with details on everything to do with the training. She had left nothing uncovered, from the strict conduct expected of all trainees to the courtesy we owed to ourselves and to the training staff.

And then, there was a little prep-up exercise. It was a prompt to reflect on why we should take the bootcamp seriously.

"But really?" I wondered, as I briefly looked through the window glass of the speeding coach at the spectacle of one London neighbourhood dropping behind to give way to another. *"Isn't it obvious why we need a hostile environment training for a trip to Baghdad?"*

The recent tragedy at the Palestine Hotel was a fresh reminder that bad things could indeed happen to any journalist putting themselves out there in Iraq. But this exercise at hand had the added wickedness of concentrating the mind, bringing to a forefront the fact that there were many other ways to die in a war zone, apart from—say—being shot at through one's hotel balcony. And it was not helpful at all to realise that even the best training in the world didn't guarantee survival.

Come to think of it, this bootcamp was just mainly a premeditated refusal to surrender blindly to fate. Humans are beasts of hope.

And what we call fate could be altered by prayer, as believers—such as myself—would readily *believe*. But fate could also be tweaked favourably by a good plan for mitigating disasters.

In that regard, astronauts going to space can teach us a thing or two about safety, even for our mundane everyday life. They may pray before being bundled into a shuttle. But at the end of the day, they never leave anything to chance.

The truth is that fortune does not just favour the brave; it also does favour those who prepare for it. So, I guess what I needed was both the training and the prayer.

At any rate, the case for this bootcamp—without which there would be no duty trip—was a reasonably strong case. There was no arguing about it with any responsible manager at the BBC. Especially, not after the BBC's John Simpson's near-encounter with tragedy, which had come shortly before that bloodiest of days for the media fraternity in Iraq—I mean, shortly before the day the Palestine Hotel was shot at.

THE SCENE FROM hell unfolded on a Sunday. It happened on 6th April 2003, this close to the fall of Baghdad. At the time, the American troops were relentlessly drilling their way towards the Iraqi capital, poking massive holes through the defence lines of those elite units of Saddam's Army. Meanwhile, in the north, another major city—Mosul, second only to Baghdad—was about to slip away from the control of the crumbling Baathist regime.

A convoy of Kurdish Peshmerga fighters and of US special forces was cutting through the heat of the day, resolutely advancing towards Mosul. Embedded in this convoy was the BBC's World Affairs Correspondent, John Simpson. It was not unlike John to be having this piece of the action. For the last half century, a tale of big trouble on the global stage seemed incomplete without John Simpson partaking in the telling of it. Tiananmen Square, the first Gulf War, Afghanistan, and countless other conflicts: John had heard the deafening fury and seen the destruction wrought by them all. And one couldn't count on him to allow any compunction—not even the fear of capture or death—to get in his way to a story.

During the war in Afghanistan, it was reported that John Simpson famously donned a *burka* to travel incognito across the border from Pakistan, playing any unsuspecting Taliban for a fool, in a demonstration of his rabidness as a story hunter. Then, there was that close call in 1991, during the Gulf War: As John filed a report from his hotel roof in Baghdad, a cruise missile flew by, skimming over his head, narrowly missing him. A *saner* human being would have spooked out, and taken off heading home. But that was not John.

John was *insane*.

In fact—to be totally candid about the veteran journalist—I would argue that it was impossible to come close to being John Simpson without scoring positively high on the psychopathy spectrum. I mean, what kind of journalist would step aside the limp and bloodied dead body of their translator and indulge in the impulsive thrill of getting on-air to report the very fatal incident?

Well, you probably wouldn't. But John did.

And John's *insanity* came with a matching dose of abundant arrogance; stuff under the urge of which he conspicuously conflated himself with the BBC—even with the United Kingdom, even with the entire Western World. John was never just a journalist working for the BBC, never just a journalist from the United Kingdom. Out there in the world, he was in himself alone *the entire BBC, the entire United Kingdom.*

See, he was the fellow who—in the wake of the

fall of Kabul in 2001—famously proclaimed to have *liberated* the Afghan capital. The fact is that journalists do not liberate cities. And if then Kabul had been liberated at all, it was by the American troops.

Understandably, John's glorious Kabul *pretension* infuriated colleagues across the BBC, especially the Bush House crowd, which was—as you may know—a cute microcosm of the world. I remember that the fellow's personal feud of sorts with Zimbabwe's Robert Mugabe had turned him into some butt of a joke within BBC Africa. Some colleagues on the news production floor—when John came over or was seen reporting on telly—called attention to him, referring to him as the *British Colonial Governor At Large*. Perhaps mean. But it underscores how some BBC staff members felt about the great reporter.

Of course, colleagues—including managing editors—were too shy to call out John Simpson in his face. And here's partly the reason why: The first time he entered a BBC building, most of us weren't born yet. John Simpson—by the way he conducted himself— seemed to have no doubt that he was the Methuselah of journalism. He had been everywhere, had seen it all. And woe betides the imprudent *infant* who might have the guts to volunteer counsel or criticism for such a character who seemed to have been living forever.

For sure, it's a painful understatement to say that John Simpson was an infliction in the backside of whoever was unfortunate enough to deal with him. Around Bush House, if anywhere, he was copiously despised.

This Sunday, 6th April 2003, John Simpson, embedded in this convoy of Kurdish Peshmerga fighters and of US special forces closing in on Mosul, would have loved to be nowhere else. And when the convoy was 20 miles away and about to enter the outskirts of the city, Simpson and his team noticed that there was a lot of military activity in the area. They were aware that there was a risk of being targeted by the US forces who were conducting airstrikes in the area against units of Saddam's Army. Credible danger was in the air.

Suddenly, just as they feared, there was a loud explosion. Something terrible just happened. And Simpson could tell that much. His four-wheeler had just taken a hit—a missile unleashed from an American F15 fighter jet.

The explosion was so powerful that the vehicle was thrown into the air, and had just landed on its side. Simpson and his team were dazed and disoriented. They quickly realised they needed to get out of the vehicle before it caught fire.

All shaking, and all covered in dust and debris, they managed to scramble out of the car. And in the wake of the settling cloud of pungent dust and debris, it quickly transpired that the attack had resulted in more than a dozen deaths. Among the dead, John Simpson's translator—Kamaran Abdurazaq Muhamed. Instant bereavement, you might think. But no, for the wounded John Simpson, bereavement over the tragic Kamaran could wait. And so, moments after the air strike, he hopped on-air and basked live in recounting how he had just escaped near-death in an American *friendly fire*. And the havoc brought about by the strike, he fittingly portrayed it as a *scene from hell*.

THE NATIONAL EXPRESS coach slowed down to a stop by a train station a little over 40 miles from London. The glow of the setting sun had set on fire the nearly-deserted platforms. Even though I was irritated by the effect on me of the passive violence of that little prep-up exercise, I still had the luxury to ponder over such a self-evident thing: Away from the hustle and bustle of London, even at 17:00 on a Friday—usually a busy time—uncrowded platforms were commonplace, out here in the country. How refreshing!

By contrast, I could mentally picture the madness of harried commuters, pouring into London Bridge at this hour, jostling into position for the next train home.

I got off the coach and dialled a minicab.

As soon as I lowered myself into the vehicle, I disappeared into my mind. And for the whole twenty-minute ride to the villa in the woods, I reviewed my practical homework for tomorrow. And yeah, I understood why I should be taking the bootcamp very seriously.

Depressingly, however, I was nagged by the

knowledge that *training* had not been enough to save John Simpson's translator; that it had not been enough to save the journalists at the Palestine Hotel's balcony.

Sad. Very sad.

However, my resolve was firmly set. I would be a good participant throughout the bootcamp. I would take away from it all I could. I was looking forward to it.

Chapter 5

CAPTAIN DORIAN SMITH

The ex-British Army officer, the cleanly-shaven *Dorian Smith,* was not *The Rock* Dwayne Johnson. But he was unquestionably a barrel of a man. Quite brawny and beefy, hard around the edges, he was convincingly a soldier, and a fitting advertisement for the job at hand.

How else would you desire your safety instructor? Flabby and soft and protruding above the belt?

No, that would have been a serious PR liability for this real-life fighter who had once seen frontline combat in the Middle East. It would have diluted his expert pronouncements in front of this naturally suspicious audience of journalists who had travelled from within Britain and from some very familiar trouble spots around the world, just to attend bootcamp.

I didn't care about the graceful aspects of Dorian's classic masculine looks. But for the sake of his authority, he was rather better this way—a hunky beefcake.

The fellow must have been in his early forties. He wasn't that tall—certainly no taller than my own six-feet. He wore no army fatigues. He was clad in a forest-coloured tee-shirt and deep-tan chinos. He was neither warm nor grumpy. He clearly was not into the humour business. Dorian was unmoved, even by the most hilarious jokes. He was immune to jokes.

Sure, for an evening companion—say, at The Cave in Soho—I would not have loved him very much. But for this crucial training on matters of life and death, Dorian was just the type one might always want in charge. There was an air of absolute believability in his earnest demeanour. His ram-rod posture and his crisp and choppy phraseology conveyed waves of energy that imbued one with a sense of safety and trust.

Dorian was now done with introducing his two wingmen to our bunch. They were *David Latham* and *Adam Cartwright.*

David was a shy fellow who stood no taller than the Captain's shoulders. He was a firearm specialist. And he would be the most active of the trio when we moved across the wooded camp out to the shooting range, where he would be performing those weapon demonstrations. As for Adam, he was the medic. He was at hand to ensure we didn't leave without any practical notion of how to handle a medical emergency.

Under his supervision, we would perform mock CPRs; we would apply tourniquets to stem mock haemorrhaging. And exceptionally, Adam would guide us through the exercise of fitting our emergency gas masks. We might need to get that right out there in Iraq, in the event of an angry and desperate Saddam unleashing upon us his infamous weapons of mass destruction. And oh, there was also the battery of real jabs he would administer—all a matter of prepping our bodies to better react to a possible bacteriological attack.

The three days would be very busy. The core of the bootcamp was the trio of instructors, but between sessions outdoors in the woods, we would repeatedly find our way back to the Spartan hallway where expert speakers from London would address us on a wide range of issues: from Wi-Fi and password security to phone hacking; from handling cash or plastic to shaking off a suspicious tail; from reading a paper map to not getting shot in a kidnap situation. It was the whole nine yards of what was needed for a safer navigation of any hostile environment.

Trainees were still munching a biscuit or downing the last draught from a Styrofoam teacup when Dorian Smith loudly clapped twice, now seeking our full attention to drive a point home.

"Before we get started, I must insist again," he said firmly: "You are—under no circumstances—to take pictures from inside or outside this venue. You will forget about this place before you leave it. You are not allowed to advertise your knowledge of it—not even vaguely the lay of the land. Certainly not any coordinates for its location."

"Why?" a trainee from Caversham asked, a little annoyed.

"Someone clearly didn't read their emails," Dorian replied, his gaze pointing nowhere near where the woman stood. "Madam, believe me. This is a matter of national security. And I'd like to be clear. If I spy any of you engaged in suspicious activity, I'll waste no time getting on the phone to your relevant manager. And before you know it, you'll be removed from the premises and sent on your way out of here. Is that fair?"

The Cavershamer didn't respond.

Like her, I thought it was all overdramatic. But it was no surprise.

I had politely been reading my emails. To me, there was nothing really unfair here. And I was certain the communal silence was no protest. It was just that journalists appreciated little—if at all—that anyone should speak to them on such an authoritative tone.

Who did Dorian Smith think he was?

Before anyone could object to the ex-serviceman, or to the way he seemed to enjoy speaking down to them, Dorian hoisted himself on the tips of his combat boots and looked past the edge of trainees to address the few fellows who still lingered in the hall.

"Guys, don't keep holding us back," he admonished

aloud. "You don't want me telling your bosses you've been poorly behaved in the woods, do you?"

It was hard to tell whether the captain might have said that in jest—Dorian was consistently unreadable. But maybe, because of his threat to snitch out the loiterers, they started streaming out and rapidly made their way forth to the rallying spot.

And now, as the captain stood there in the back lawn of the English countryside villa, setting the agenda for the day, with his back turned to the woods, the semi-circle of his attentive audience accrued. The tardy ones ultimately rallied the ranks.

"Remember," Dorian said solemnly, "we have only one goal at heart for the next three days: to ensure you don't get killed or kidnapped out there in the dangerous world, if what it will take to stay alive is a good training." The words of the captain seemed to land with a crashing finality. And as though he had knocked his audience into that stunning silence, our bunch stood politely quiet—quiet in unison.

"To hit our goal," Dorian went on, "I ask you to pay attention; to participate. And for just these three days, you will have to set your reporter's mindset aside. Don't be argumentative. Let us do our work. Yes—we demand complete discipline. Once you are out there, it will possibly make the difference between life and death. Literally."

As I listened to the captain, I slowly decided that I liked him. He would have made for a fascinating interview subject. Clearly, his years in the Army had not been a waste.

AS A BBC broadcaster, when someone like my boss, Kari Blackburn, asked me what I would do when I ultimately grew tired of the daily grind of our trade, I had a ready answer to provide: Go into traditional academia and teach journalism to the next generation of media professionals; or open my own Media Academy in Kigali and cater to professionals of all backgrounds; professionals with a need to understand and work with the media. Now, I had never had a reason to wonder what servicemen did when they were tired of life in the barracks and then decided to part ways with the British Army. I could easily have guessed that some went on to become mercenaries, guided by anything but classic morality, always ready to turn themselves into guns for hire. A cliché, of course!

I now know that there is a high demand for ex-military personnel in the private security industry. But before this encounter with Dorian Smith and his wingmen, I would have been mostly guessing if I had tried to talk to anyone about this. Dorian Smith opened my eyes to the fact that there are many decent ways for ex-military personnel to turn their military experience into another rewarding career. Some ex-military personnel go to Hollywood to work as stuntmen or as story consultants for movie studios. Others recycle themselves in the media, being paid a generous salary to provide TV networks with expert insights into military matters. The transition into broadcasting and journalism can sometimes be radical, but it is more common than one might think.

In that regard, only a few cases could be as illustrative as that of Josh Rushing, today the host of the *Fault Lines* show on *Al-Jazeera English*. Of all the places where he could have ended up, Al-Jazeera was the unlikeliest for this American. And here is why:

Josh had served for fourteen years in the US Marine Corps and was deployed as the US military's lead spokesperson to the Arab World as part of the invasion of Iraq. In that role, as a self-styled *willing salesman of the cause*, he participated in spinning America's narrative of the conflict, repeating what he called *an honestly believed assurances of our unselfish motives*.

As it were, Josh was fully in character—playing his spin-doctoring part—when he sat down for an interview with the producers of *Control Room*, a dramatic documentary on the media and the invasion of Iraq. The film would shoot him to fame and to a change of professional path. But back then, in his role as army mouthpiece, the blue-eyed Texan would rattle out one variant or another of a carefully rehearsed spiel:

> *We are not here to occupy an Arab land,* Josh Rushing would say; *we are not here to take your oil; we are not here to kill Arabs, to take*

*mosques... we are here to fight terrorists. And
if we don't fight them here, we will have to
fight them home.*

Gaslighting was part of waging wars in the name of Uncle Sam. And dear Josh Rushing was a dexterous gaslighter at the time American bombs were killing Arabs in Baghdad and beyond.

After the release of *Control Room*—and when the lie about the war became so obvious that any deliberate cognitive dissonance could no longer be entertained at any reasonable measure—Josh underwent a change of heart: At the end of his six-month tour in the Middle East, he would go home knowing somewhat better about the Arabs. The educated fellows he had chatted up in Qatar didn't want to blow him to pieces. They had dreams, hopes, and fears. Just like his folks in Texas. From their perspective as non-Americans at the receiving end of American imperialism, their anger made sense. Josh thus had gone home with conflicted feelings about the gap of what he knew about American democratic ideals and what America would do abroad in the name of its grand hegemonic interests.

But what could he do at a personal level?

Well, Josh would later go back to the frontline. This time, a different frontline—The Arab and global audiences he had contributed to mislead and to gaslight, he was now determined to enlighten. As a broadcaster.

Before taking his seat as host of *Fault Lines*, the ex-marine published a book, *Mission Al-Jazeera*, about his early days in his new role. In the book, he discusses —without revealing much—the issues he was not allowed to touch upon, when he was in the official employ of the US Army. The tone of the book was moderate, reserved. In the book, he was quite the diplomat. But to hell with all that—how dare he ever defect to the *Arab enemy*?

How dare he?

Sean Hannity, the gloriously infamous host of *Fox News*, would brand him a traitor. And that was of course in a complete dismissal of the rather humanistic terms of Josh's new mission: *Build a bridge, seek the truth, change the world.*

Unfazed by the criticism, however, the ex-marine would sail on and settle into his post-Marine-Corps life. His new job would take him to places all over the world: From Iraq to Colombia; from Vietnam to North Dakota, etc. And in these places, he would turn on the camera and shoot hard-hitting specials and documentaries, exploring previously untold stories of great human interests, of great human tragedies. Apart from the fact that *Al-Jazeera English* is a foreign media outlet, which had sparked a bit of patriotic fury when it entered the US cable market, Josh Rushing was no exception in his professional transition. In fact, the examples are legions. Thomas Gibbons-Neff of the *New York Times* is another marine-turned-journalist.

Thomas had served two combat tours in Afghanistan before returning to the country as a media operative, initially for *The Washington Post*. After the fall of Afghanistan in August 2021, in the wake of Joe Biden's decision to cut and run, Thomas undertook one very unusual assignment that must not have sat well with the *Sean Hannities* of the world. In a building that had been refurbished by the Americans a couple of years earlier and was now the headquarters of the new Taliban regime, he lowered down to his haunches for an interview with a Taliban commander.

Nothing intriguing in itself. But here's the kicker: Eleven years earlier, that very Taliban commander attacked the company of Marines, in which Gibbons-Neff was a corporal.

I mean, if any test was needed to show that the professional transition of the ex-infantryman was successfully complete, that was it.

While the marine he had been would have killed the commander at the earliest opportunity, the reporter he had become just wanted a chat with him; he just wanted to understand him. And he would not have minded breaking bread with him, had that been indispensable in establishing rapport to get him talking. Gibbons's interview with the Taliban commander was a classic journalist's stunt, wonderfully pulled off by an ex-soldier.

NOW, WHAT IF—UPON leaving the army—one desired to remain within familiar territory, risking no such thing as being branded a traitor, for palling around with Talibans, or for turning the camera on America to feed a show on an Arab television network?

Captain Dorian Smith might never have bothered with such a question or worried about being abused by some British Conservative media hosts for his choice of career path after the barracks. Perhaps, he was no man with a taste for the limelight.

But one thing was certain: If not a stuntman, a Hollywood story consultant, or a war reporter, Dorian Smith—with that gift of the gab he had got going on—could have made for a wonderful military analyst on British national television.

But obviously, he had gone for something much closer to home: using his military expertise to inform his new career as a safety and security coach; one who got media correspondents ready for deployment to war zones. I was grateful to have him on bootcamp.

Chapter 6

TRAINING DAY

Day three of bootcamp started just like the previous two days—with tea, coffee, and pretty palatable croissants in the dining lounge. Up next, we poured out into the grounds of the camp. Like yesterday, we were out again in foul weather under a patched grey sky.

After tea, the drills came fast: fake press conference, fake discovery of a mass grave, fake mysterious source offering to sell secrets.

Today, we would cram in everything left on the agenda, being tested in practice on what we had mostly discussed in theory. This was the busiest of the three days. We were getting down and dirty. And at some point, we were told to get ready for what came next. Shortly thereafter, an explosion rang out. A simulation.

But a real explosion, with a rising cloud of smoke. Bear in mind: This was an actual training facility of the British Armed forces. Recruits for special branches of the Police borrowed it from time to time. They had everything in this camp for wonderful pyrotechnics, and for all kinds of other stunts.

Throughout the bootcamp, a small army of human props could act very mean on demand, changing sets of outfits to become terrorists, enemy combatants, regular army guys, or corrupt functionaries at checkpoints speaking in very bad English and demanding payment in U.S. dollars for missing paperwork that could not be produced because it did not exist. It was all drilling, but everything we simulated could happen in the real world.

Back to that explosion.

In the wake of it, there were reports of casualties—reports by bloody survivors who had emerged out of the woods, panting, and absolutely looking rough. As part of the brief for the drill, a newswire crew, spotted near the scene, was whisked away in a van; editors were calling up for details, wanting the story on-air.

In groups of *fours*, we were assigned to deal with the incident. To run a standard risk assessment, make a judgement call, report on it safely without compromise to editorial integrity. All under a tight deadline. My group opted to play it safe; we retreated into the countryside villa, which would have been our hotel if this had been for real out there in Baghdad. One group set out to locate the scene of the explosion and ended up captives, their release made conditional upon the payment of a ransom.

Another group, also out to the scene, took fire from men in black balaclavas—hooded men who then took off, shouting Death to America. All in all, this drill, like the others, was staged to strike as close to reality as possible and elicit adrenaline rushes, testing our toughness to survive similar real-life hostility.

"YOU FAILED TO demonstrate to your newsroom back at base the benefit of having you in the field," Captain Dorian told my squad. "Remember, you are not on holidays guys. Your default move should not be to just give up on the story."

We were stumped. And we weren't the only group who opted to play it safe—two other groups also did. As far as responding to this situation went, our option was admittedly a low hanging fruit. But most often, the simplest is the best. Ockham's razor stuff

"What's wrong with choosing safety?" enquired a male voice. The speaker, a sinewy red-haired camera operator, continued: "That explosion screamed danger, Captain. And some news crew got kidnapped—crucial detail we couldn't ignore. How could ours possibly be the wrong call?"

Captain Dorian spun around and fixed a deadpan gaze at the young man. "I like your passion. Now, what do you think? Did you make the right call?"

I wrestled against the temptation to jump in, and ultimately decided not to interfere, wanting to see where this was headed.

And as we stared at our spokesman, gauging his determination, he unflinchingly said, "Yes, we made the right call. Well, under those precise circumstances."

Dorian remained placid. "How was that the right call?"

"Well—" the camera guy drew a blank. And he appeared to remember a line we'd heard far too often since all of this started. "No story is worth dying for," he announced, cocking his head aside, rubbing his neck as though to ease some tension there.

"But what reason did you have to fear death?"

He scoffed impatiently.

Then: "The groups who ventured out near the scene, how did it pan out for them? Guys scored a kidnapping. Terrible. And I bet there's nothing really to brag about having been shot by a bunch of anti-American nutjobs. Do we wish we were kidnapped or shot at? I don't think so."

"Okay," the captain cut in. "When you are deployed to a war zone, it's not far-fetched to expect you could be kidnapped or shot."

"What's your point, though?" our red-haired pal shrugged. "I don't understand."

"The groups you refer to, they did a good job in how they handled the kidnapping and the shooting casualties. Caught up in their terrible predicament, it all came down to how they would react. And the way they responded doesn't suggest their training was ineffective."

"Still, they got kidnapped. And shot at!"

The assembly laughed. Captain Smith didn't.

"But no one ended up dead," the captain said. "And this is my point."

What was the catch? I wondered. *Was there just one way to run this drill?*

"No one ended up dead, yes," our spokesman agreed, remaining defiant. "But the best outcome is not to get shot at or kidnapped in the first place. Our group made the right call. And why? Again, no story is worth the risk dying for."

"Well done!" Dorian exclaimed, conceding at last with a grin—a rare grin.

The young man chuckled. "You almost got me worked up. And for what?" And with that, he elicited another guffaw from the assembly.

Dorian took half a step toward him. And giving him a firm handshake, he said: "I just wasn't sure how convinced you were about the soundness of your call. I love your reasoning. And yes, if we were to pick a motto for this training, this would be it—*No bloody story is worth dying for.*"

Chapter 7

THE SHOOTING RANGE

I fidgeted with unreserved apprehension when the slew of jabs was punched into my blood stream. Along with the modelling of those gas masks, the whole thing was occupational health *on steroids*. It would be a lie to tell you I was comfortable with this chemical invasion of my body.

But it wasn't optional. The alternative was to back away from the duty trip—to stay away from Iraq, altogether.

Sister Wong—the BBC's in-house occupational health specialist for Bush House—had told me it was all for our greater good. And *Adam Latham* had echoed Mrs Wong when he reassured us it was all safe. As Adam put it, the jabs were intended to build us up to survive a possible exposure to those bloody weapons of mass destruction. They were a second-line defence of sorts. The first line?

Well, that was each of these hideous gas masks. Trying the mask on, practicing the fitting of it around my head was both fun and unsettling at the same time. Until now, I had only seen or read about gas masks in films and books. It now felt surreal having one in my hands.

As we arrived at the shooting range, *David*—the firearm specialist—made a point of reminding us, before he got down to work, that we should not be complacent and ignore any persistent feeling of unease.

"A bit of fever is expected," he said, as he handed us earmuffs. "But it becomes a matter for the doctors at A&E if you experience an unusually violent reaction. Or if the fever extends beyond 48 hours."

Now, I was really scared. "*What have I done?*" I wondered, feeling reckless for having allowed these *poisons* into my veins.

However, I immediately cut myself some slack, taking solace from the fact that I was not alone; from the fact that a bunch of other BBC staffers—already in the Middle East—had safely gone through this.

"Guys," David Latham called, "you are officially under my care for the next two hours. And all of this little reminder is just standard protocol. You will be fine."

Warning us very sternly to keep our earmuffs in place for the sake of our eardrums, David—switching from a weapon of a certain grade to another—took aim at some dummy targets and blasted them away.

That went on for a while.

Next, David took us through the boring subjects of firearms and firearm calibres, and then through a cute story about the deceptive nature of gun reports.

"The noise of a gun says very little about where its bullet might be travelling," David said at some point, after he had pushed the muffs clear off his head. "When you are running for safety, do not trust the direction of the sound, which is likely to be that of the wind. It might lead you straight into the shooter. A possible deadly trap."

I never thought of a gun report from this perspective. For sure, I always understood the sound of warfare in terms of heavy artillery and light weaponry. That's how journalists often inferred judgement about the intensity of a battle.

Sure, David's chatter was boring. But David was saying things. And his concern was to empower us to read the acoustics of warfare for safety purposes. I was sure learning stuff.

"Also good to know," the firearms expert went on, "bullets always travel faster than the sound. Good news is, when you have heard the gun report, you are still alive. You then have to make the most of it."

He didn't mean to be funny.

But it was funny, by the way he said it.

"You don't survive a bullet to only end up with

the rotten luck of running in the wrong direction. Here's the point: even amid the maddening staccato of fire, don't do knee-jerk stuff. Don't just think about running. If it's safe to do so, stay low. Assess before safely getting out of harm's way."

And so, David Latham lectured on.

Just when I started to think David Latham was talking too much, he paused to solicit questions. And he got a barrage of questions about all aspects of the weaponry of modern warfare.

And mine was a pesky one. It had lingered in my mind, unsettling me as much as did the matter of the gas masks and those jabs.

"You have not said much about weapons of mass destruction," I politely told David, when he saw my raised hand and gestured for me to speak. "The talk in town is all about WMDs."

"That's true," someone concurred. "Are they as scary as they sound?"

"Weapons of mass destruction!" David said slowly, pensive for a moment. "The sound of it frightens the hell out of us all. And rightfully so. But we often do not hear what it truly means."

For the next fifteen minutes, as David embarked on lecturing us on the nature of weapons of mass destruction, I started to understand that the way politicians casually threw the expression around was mainly intended for shock purposes—for propaganda. You want to make the devil look even more devilish;

you want to call him Belzebuth, and enjoy watching how little kids would squirm.

"A weapon of mass destruction," David said, "is a type of weapon that is undiscriminating. Unlike a bullet, weapons of mass destruction may kill more than the intended target. For example, while a gun is not technically a weapon of mass destruction, a can of mustard gas is. Mustard gas does not care what it is aimed at. A gas will spread throughout and kill anyone in its path. It does not matter if the person in its path is a civilian or a high priest."

"Well," I said, "wouldn't a machine gun qualify as a WMD? Mass shooting has often featured in the news."

"No, I am afraid," the expert disagreed. "A mass shooter needs to fire repeatedly if his gun doesn't do so automatically. But each of his bullets will still shoot straight forward. Even a thousand bullets won't spread the way mustard gas would."

By the time David wrapped up his lecture, I felt stupid for ever overlooking this: The deadliest weapon of mass destruction ever used since the dawn of time was by the USA—the atomic bomb in Hiroshima and Nagasaki. Of course, that is a fact of History I have always known. I just never thought of the atomic bomb in terms of "weapon of mass destruction." Oh, how could I ever have overlooked that?

THE FOLLOWING MORNING, after three days of bootcamp, I went back to London. Courtesy of the training, I now felt confident about my survival skills. If anything, I was better in administrating CPR. But there was more.

There was in me this newfound clarity—The possession of weapons of mass destruction was no problem in itself. But if you were Saddam Hussein, with one George W. Bush as President in the United States of America, the very hint that you might have these bloody weapons was an irredeemable sin.

Chapter 8

THIS VAGUE SENSE OF MENACE

The clock had long been on the lighter side of what was left of the night when I awoke this Tuesday. The flight was scheduled to board at 4:35 PM, nearly twelve hours away. But I couldn't take sleep any further. Sleep was always elusive before a trip like this one. Even for an ordinary assignment—one that did not entail such a credible possibility of being killed—I often felt restive until the plane was up in the air. And that came at a cost.

It got in the way of proper slumber. There was always the nagging fear that I might be leaving something behind: a bullet-proof vest, a passport, an editorial brief, an accreditation, a trimmer, the batteries for the *B-GAN* satellite kit.

If only deceptively, to arise early—earlier than the

sun—offered an assurance that I would be thorough and would leave nothing crucial behind. Imagine plodding through the London traffic and getting to Heathrow Airport at thirty miles away to realise that the travel papers under the lampshade in the home study had stayed there. Oh, that would land like a punch. So, I had my reasons to be on my feet now, to be up this early. Perhaps, I would take a nap later in the day. Now, beyond the glare of artificial vapour light, I picked out the silent advance of dawn. If I needed to be sure, I could have gone outside and looked at the sky. From my front lawn, looking up past the privet hedge, I could have read the progress of the early morning in the slowly growing spill of orange that was closing in from the east.

But the mere glance at that clock, which had rung to wake me up, was quite enough. In any event, I could rely on the common knowledge that daybreaks in the spring are notoriously impatient; the Sun in the spring is more aggressive about climbing out of its nest as if it would be damned to delay its rise until eight or nine, as it does in the winter.

Anyway, I was now out of bed. And as I took a quick shower to rinse away the remnants of sleep, and then moved on to take an ultimate stock of the items I had packed for the trip, I could sense that dawn was predictably coming fast. And that was fine.

I am not afraid of the light. So, I was certain— beyond a doubt—that the looming daybreak was none of the reason why I felt the weight of this heavy and unpleasant knot in the pit of my stomach; this sentiment of imperceptible menace, which seemed to have yanked some rug of safety from under my feet.

This unease, I knew of course what it was.

I certainly couldn't put it down to something that might have changed overnight in Thamesmead; everything I knew about Thamesmead was the same as it had been before I went to bed last evening. An ordinary evening in Thamesmead had little or nothing in common with where I will be headed later today, where I would dangerously be spending the nights in the coming days.

Thamesmead was not Baghdad.

And perhaps, I should elaborate on that.

WHEN DISCUSSING BRITAIN, especially away from the *Island*, I have occasionally found it useful to parlay faces and places from popular tales into emotional hallmarks, providing a sense of familiarity where there evidently might be none. Fans of Charles Dickens' *A Christmas Carol* often feel like they know Camden Town. Likewise, those who saw *Paddington*—the film about the bear from Darkest Peru—or read the original book by Michael Bond may similarly swear that they have somehow had a real-life experience in connection with that London rail station where they could catch an express train to Heathrow Airport.

I certainly enjoy contemplating the glimmer of light that would illuminate a face in Brussels or Baghdad when I unoriginally suggest that, once in London, one should visit the collection of celebrity waxworks at *Madame Tussaud*, which I would delicately place just round a corner from the old quarters of Sherlock Holmes in Baker Street. Yes—It is corny, I know.

One might never have been to London, but tell me: Who is yet to learn about the most famous Victorian detective?

I mean, calling upon the fictional sleuth and then placing him in location—either at home, or out and about doing what he does best—breeds a believable sense of familiarity.

Problem is, the exercise nearly fails me when I attempt to point such a virtual connection to my own neighbourhood in London: Thamesmead is not prominent on your usual travel guide. The official guidebook very likely won't be useful in taking you to Thamesmead. And you are even less likely to end up in Thamesmead thanks to a Sherlock-Holmes-related storyline—There simply is no such a storyline.

For all the time he had plied his trade out of *221B Baker Street*, Sherlock Holmes seemed to have been everywhere in the capital to investigate a crime, to probe a mystery. Except Thamesmead, apparently. To the Victorians, for sure, if Thamesmead had been anything yet, it must have arguably been more *Kent* than *London*.

Thamesmead, located twelve miles southeast of the City of London, was a world apart. But thanks to the never-ending human impulse to urbanise and to *develop*, administrative division in Britain is quite of a different thing today. If the detective were somehow to return to Baker Street, he will have to update his records if—as expected—he would petulantly stick to depending on his mindpower rather than the power of this dependable modern system that we call *Google Maps*.

In any event, the closest Sherlock Holmes ever came to my neighbourhood was Blackheath and Woolwich Arsenal, in today's Royal Borough of Greenwich. The detective had been in Blackheath for the case of *The Norwood Builder,* which was about the presumed murder of one Jonas Oldacre, an obnoxious fellow who was notorious for once having *let a cat loose in a bird sanctuary*. In the end, Oldacre was flushed out as the villain in the story of his own murder, which naturally wasn't a murder at all. The probe into his malicious little scheme was Holmes's first adventure after his *return*, following the tragic demise of Professor Moriarty, his nemesis. And Woolwich Arsenal, Sherlock visited thereafter to probe the death of the mysterious Cadogan West. Serious government business was at stake in that matter. And it was at the request of Holmes's brother, Mycroft, that he had thus returned to the borough to dig into the conundrum. His loyal companion—the affable and womanising Dr Watson—had called it *The Adventure of The Bruce-Partington Plans*. And yes, this case was the one that took Sherlock Holmes closest to home, closest to Thamesmead.

Now, what would I roughly tell a stranger in Baghdad—if only anecdotally—about the fact that Thamesmead never offered itself for the kind of uncanny business that would have brought the detective along, running and drooling over the prospect of sinking a tooth into a bloody mystery?

Well, Thamesmead is one relatively safe neighbourhood. You won't find it, say, on the *London map* of knife crime. Sure, it is no Garden of Eden. But there, the occasional emergency vehicle cruising down the main street is not a squad car from Scotland Yard racing to a crime scene; it's likely to be an ambulance, from the nearby Queen Elisabeth Hospital, making a dash to an address in a bid to snatch a resident from the jaws of a cardiac arrest, or from an unusually nasty fall at home.

See, that's why Sherlock Holmes would never have stood a chance if he wanted a reason to visit. Though more accurately, it was because the ex-Greater London Council was not yet a thing and could obviously not have started its work to turn the area into that extension of what was then known as *The Royal Arsenal*.

More to the point, it wasn't until the mid-1960s— long after Queen Victoria and the *celebrated Sherlock Holmes*—that Thamesmead set out on its way to becoming *Thamesmead* and was then hailed rather bombastically as a *Town of Tomorrow*. In such an old country as England, Thamesmead is perfectly a *new* little town.

Tucked somewhere over an area of formerly neglected marshland between the River Thames and the north-eastern edge of neighbouring Abbey Wood, Thamesmead could in fact claim to be a world apart and away from the busy streets of Central London. That may however be changing rapidly.

The forces of gentrification have been on its case over the last few years. With the *Cross Rail—the Elisabeth Line*—which has now placed it at a mere fifteen minutes from the old business districts, the area has been getting busier and busier, more and more select. Today, new construction sites are a familiar sight throughout Thamesmead—Men are at work *the best part of the week* to future-proof the town, to dress it up with more glitter and glamour. Naturally, every aspect of life in Thamesmead is now set to come at a higher premium, for it has now become a *new frontier* for property hunters; an attractive destination for office workers who—among a long roll of other things—would appreciate a short stroll to the wood surrounding the ruins of *Lesnes Abbey*, where the smell of lush pine trees and the rhapsodies of tweeting birds would wash away the stress brought upon by the previous days of the daily grind.

And that is Thamesmead, today.

But Thamesmead was different at the time of the Iraq War. It was even more different when I moved into my street in the latest half of the 1990s. Back then, the neighbourhood was openly unapologetic about its rustic beginnings. Visitors coasting down the bridge straddling the railway and overlooking the local station to the left, were unavoidably greeted by the sight of grazing stable horses in the front lawns of the sprawling council estate that stood at the *original heart* of the new town. It wasn't yet urban enough for white-collar commuters who did their *nine-to-five* at the Square Mile or elsewhere. At the same time, to the fox-hunting type—to the typical card-carrying member of the *Countryside Alliance*—Thamesmead wasn't *countryside* enough: In its hybrid identity, it was rather an annoying disgrace for anyone who was fan of the *rifle* and *game*. It didn't even have any allotments for growing vegetables on a sizeable scale, let alone any hunting grounds—not even this long before Tony Blair closed in with his ban on fox-hunting.

Now, to the locals—to us—all was fine with *The Mead. The Mead* was as good as it came. And the semi-provincial quality of the neighbourhood accounted much for its charm. For one thing, we properly greeted our neighbours, in contrast to the fake smiles and superficial interactions that are all too common in the London Square Mile.

Above all, of course, Thamesmead—again, though not a Garden of Eden—basked in a rarity of crime.

Yeah, at a time when, say, in Peckham, in Woolwich Arsenal, a casual weekend errand exposed anyone to police flyers warning against *violent yobs operating in this area,* or to notices calling for possible witnesses to a fatal stabbing the previous night; at such a time of serious safety concerns elsewhere, Thamesmead was relatively a haven.

Relatively.

And I quite liked Thamesmead as it was.

THIS EARLY MORNING of April, there had been no report of the imminent falling of an asteroid over Thamesmead, of a fatal stabbing at the town's main junction, of a Jack the Ripper on the prowl, of an unusual string of break-ins in the neighbourhood. Still, I felt heavy, hollow, and ungrounded; and going through the motion of ultimately checking my travel gears did nothing to distract me.

What was the matter?

Oh, I knew what the matter was.

My three items of luggage were now ready; the tickets, the passport and the press pass were together in a brief tucked into my carry-on; the cab for the airport had been booked nearly twenty-four hours earlier. I mean, this bloody duty trip was indeed happening; and as the minutes ticked away, with the time to bid farewell inching forth with every tick, I was already in Baghdad in harm's way. I was already there, in spirit. So, I knew what the matter was. And it was not the looming daybreak. Again, I am not scared of the light. And no, Thamesmead where I was still shuttling in and out of my living room was as safe as I knew it to be.

This is rather what I didn't want to confront: The Palestine Hotel, at the heart of Baghdad where I had already mentally checked in; right there—as I knew from the events earlier in the month—the hypothetical falling asteroid, the Ripper on the prowl, the stab from the knife-wielding yob could assume the shape of a high-explosive round from an American M1A1 Abrams tank smashing in through a façade of concrete and steel and glass, leaving death in its wake.

For a moment, as chaos flashed in my mind, I scolded myself for this slide-back into cowardice—the cowardice of drawing such morbid plans, visualising doom. Then, I tried to rationalise my fear away as I had done a few times previously. I told myself: *You have been kidding yourself lately, acting courageous. But this is not irrational at all—this is war, and you are no stranger to what happens in a war.*

My attempt at calming myself didn't help!

What it did was to open a gateway to a bigger demon. For briefly there, my mind chartered me back to 1994—Back to Rwanda in April 1994, amidst the madness of the incipient *100 Days of Terror*. But before any of those fear-stricken faces returned into full focus and impaired me by assuming their haunting quality, I stemmed this flux of disheartening memories.

No, this was a terrible moment for such a recall; to dwell there any second longer would be crippling. I had no use for this dead weight. Especially, now.

But where would I hang my mind, which had thus decided to run riot?

See, the girls and their mother had stayed up late to help with the packing. If I woke them up now, we could talk, and I wouldn't be thinking about Baghdad. But it wouldn't vanquish my anxieties. We might still discuss the trip without touching on what made it problematic. As you know, to address the elephant in the room is uncomfortable enough; but it is outright distressing to disregard the elephant in the room because we *hate the discomfort* of openly addressing it.

Anyway, the girls and their mother were yet to arise. They knew my flight wasn't due for boarding until 4:35 p.m. And before they awoke around seven and walked in here, my restive mind flashed again forward to the hotel. And as though by a curse, it went straight back to shooting the same film: *The high-explosive round smashing in through the façade of concrete and steel and glass, leaving death in its wake.* As it were, my graphic knowledge of the blunder from *the Jumhuria* Bridge was my trouble—a burden, in which this sentiment of imperceptible menace found its roots. And as it happened, this very burden of *knowing* gave a distinct aspect of *suicide mission* to all of this. This Goddamn *back-slide* gave an air of bereavement to what I did next—I mean, the farewell.

Chapter 9

ONE IMPORTANT GOODBYE

A little after 7:30 a.m., the last in the family to throw off the bedsheets was on her feet. Mum and the girls filed in downstairs to trade a *good morning*. Their eyes silently scanned the room, inspecting the neatly-packed pieces of luggage. They knew what they were.

Among the pile was the boring and large suitcase, the type much familiar to any traveller leaving home for at least a month. It held the clothes and the shoes and the brushes—all those mundane items. Then every other pack, tagged with eye-catching *white-on-blue* stickers, screamed *British Broadcasting Corporation*. Most notable of all was the black heavy-duty hardcase. It enclosed most of the load. In fact, it packed a portable mini studio, complete with a mixer, a pair of microphones, a sat-phone gear, a safety reporter's vest. If I arrived in the field without the massive black hardcase, I would be completely hamstrung—a useless special envoy, one with no homing device to keep in touch with the *Control Room* at Bush House.

Of course, from the contents of the black standard BBC backpack—the other most important piece of luggage in the pile—I would still have my handheld newsgathering kit: a mini-disc recorder, a sound monitor, and a unidirectional microphone. Also, from the same standard backpack, I would still have the BBC *standard-issue* laptop. It was loaded with all the production-specific pieces of software, which normally allowed BBC reporters in remote locations to stay connected with *and on top* of what the team at base was up to.

But without the mini studio and without the gear for the satellite link-up, I would still be an *editorial castaway*. Even if I ran into the scoop of the century, I would be beaten to it by hungrier colleagues who would stand ready with highly operational gears close at hand.

I didn't readily bore Dedeli and the girls with the technical details of my job or of this particular duty trip. But the BBC and its related business paid the bills in the house. With time, the family had come to understand even some of the most unspoken aspects of what it was to be a BBC journalist. So, as they reviewed my collection of gears, they knew that each piece of apparent *junk* must be there if my assignment were to be successful. And seeing that they were all neatly packed, they could tell Daddy was ready. But for now, they would say nothing about the trip. There would be time for that after shower, after breakfast.

I PLAYED IT cool and unfazed. Because a worried look on a parent's face—a look that draws inordinate attention from a child—is never fair. Children, to the extent of what's possible, should always be allowed to be carefree. I certainly didn't want to burden the girls with my angst. Dad had the parental duty to be the *rock*. So, I wore a deceptively upbeat face when Isaro—now ready to depart for school—sauntered up to me and threw her tender delicate hands around my neck.

"Good luck, papa," she said in that innocent voice of hers as we locked up in a hug. "I love you, and I'll miss you."

The feel of her vulnerable body in my arms—this little creature who still required a Dad for protection and for her emotional comfort—caused me to well inside with tension. I offered a silent prayer and decided that I ought to get back to her alive. No, I couldn't accept this hug as our last ever. And as I let her go and she walked away with Mum on their way to school, I prayed again.

Oh, prayer!

Prayer is a mysterious business. We do all we can in trying times for the best possible outcome. Yet, the possibility of things going against us never goes away.

But with prayer, that possibility is erased from our mind. And gone with it are those unpleasant feelings, the insidious seeds of doubt and indecisiveness. Prayer reminds us that those tragedies waiting to happen are but disquieting thoughts on close examination.

Sure, I deeply respect those who can do without prayer. Good for them. But I am grateful there is such a thing as what I like to call the *comforting science of prayer*. It relaxes me when I am tense. And in this case, it draped me with the softening assumption of a safe return home, even as I was yet to leave; even as I could see a few scenarios, whereby I might actually never return.

Good luck, papa, Isaro's voice resounded again in my mind.

And in my mind, I said *amen*!

Her younger sister Astrida had been the first to go through the motions last night. I had already tucked myself up in bed, getting ready to struggle for those few hours of sleep when she shyly walked into our bedroom. Again, I did my best to downplay the risks of the assignment. But she couldn't be fooled. She was a child. But she understood enough to know that I was honey-coating this thing.

"Take care of yourself, papa," she said, wearing her concern on her face, her usual childish insouciance now nowhere on display. "I love you."

Her *I-love-you* landed harshly, rather hitting me as an injunction. Before Isaro later came to drive that reminder home when we hugged, I grasped the full weight of my ponderous duty to survive Iraq—I couldn't afford to die in Baghdad; my seven-year-old didn't deserve to be deprived of countless other occasions to proclaim her *love* to Daddy. And with the weight of that thought, I certainly could not have slept as soundly as I desired.

EXCEPT IN CASES of emergency, I don't make any social call before 9:00 a.m. Before 9:00 AM, most people are still setting up their day. Handling a social call is not very likely to feature as their priority.

As it were, I didn't place my first call out until the sun was riding high enough in its morning ascent. And at 10:00 a.m. past, before I continued with running down that list of friends and relatives whom I was yet to say goodbye to, I remembered this *one important goodbye* that must not be conducted at a distance—my farewell to Pat and Ted. The silver-haired octogenarian couple was a testament to the general *welcoming* spirit of the Brits. They were the neighbours who went out of their way to induct me into Thamesmead when I turned up in the area in 1997. I could write a volume just to extol their doting brand of kindness. But I shall simply say that Ted and Pat shared a great deal with me, including their knowledge of the area and its people, including their values of not looking down on others.

The couple voted *Labour*. They naturally saw to it

that I was soon familiar with the tenets of the *Labour Party*. As a new Londoner, I inherited their fascination with the charismatic Tony Blair who had just pitched up a tent at 10 Downing Street.

Tell you what?

Family, indeed, can be more than just a story of blood relation. With Ted and Pat, I have known that to be resoundingly true. Having lost my father in the Rwandan Tragedy, I had found in Ted a father figure, and in Pat a *mum*.

Sure, my mum was still alive, never far off in my heart, though she lived at 12,000 miles away in the Country of a Thousand Hills.

Yeah, no one could replace her in my universe. But in London, Pat was the *Other Mother*—the white mother I never thought I would ever have.

That altered my whole approach to the eternally thorny issue of race. It was a real-life school which taught me that we are always guaranteed to be wrong when we put a haste in reading the world as a giant binary black-and-white stage.

Long story short, Pat and Ted had been part of my family since 1997. At home, a Christmas or a birthday would not have been complete without the calming and reassuring silhouettes of Ted and Pat—two lovely souls who were an effective advertisement for old age.

Of course, the couple was the first outside the BBC to know about my assignment to the war zone. And of course, they were concerned. All the ugliness about

Iraq was there on telly for them to see. They knew that anyone travelling there was a potential casualty. And now, at 10:00 a.m. past, I had just walked up to their doorsteps and rang the bell.

"Venuste," Ted called with a smile as the door opened, and he reached out to give me that usual hug. "It's *today!?*"

When we let go of our brief embrace, I said: "Yes, it's today—Baghdad is calling!" Along the way, I tried not to sound sombre. But the atmosphere took an immediate air of sombreness all the same, for Ted glared at me but immediately had nothing to say. Instead, he leaned again forward and spoke with his body. He offered me a new hug, which seemed to have *opened him up* as he suddenly had the inspiration for some good small talk.

And we talked for a while.

"You have to go, Venuste," Ted said, after nothing significant was left for us to cover. "But please, take good care of yourself."

In Teddy's subsequent struggle not to tear up, he unwittingly brought me to tears. Yeah, like a little boy, and with my eyes lingering on his gentle frame, I shamelessly burst into tears.

"You'll be back, Venuste," he comforted. "You will." And this time, Ted sounded more resolute, perhaps having realised that joining me in this business of *moistening up* would be counter-productive. And since we both had no use for drawing out this emotionally-taxing farewell, we shook hands within five minutes of my arrival. Ted quietly disappeared behind the door while I pensively retraced my steps.

And as I made my way back to my living room strewn with those traveller's packs, I caught myself thinking about the rest of those people I had to call. Then, I caught myself thinking about the ordeal of the afternoon's traffic that lay in wait on my way to Heathrow Airport.

Chapter 10

THE SCENT OF HEATHROW

The weather and the traffic were rather depressing. Right upon our exit from the *Black Wall Tunnel*, the slow jams started. And by now, the clear morning had turned into something grey, something wet. Yes, there was rain. Not a fine drizzle. But a draping downpour. That was fine. For this was London. So, that was fine.

Anyway, after about two hours of slog through the traffic jams and through the curtain of steady downpour, the stubbled and rather tall cab driver slid under a tunnel for the umpteenth time. Then, came a break in the monotony that had settled between us. And what was that? First, a word about the cabbie: The fellow could have been Moroccan, Turkish, or even Venezuelan. I didn't ask for clarification.

Nothing warranted it. As far as I can tell, unwarranted conversations about *origins* are minefields sometimes. They can potentially trigger violent feelings, or appalling memories. Not everyone left home the last time hugging loved ones and smiling away into the horizon. And I know the *hell* what I am talking about. I really do.

So, I systematically avoid conversations about *origins* where nothing relevant calls for them. However, my observant eyes are never idle—and often, as I observe—I take mental or written notes. For a journalist, that comes with the territory.

All the way since we departed Thamesmead, the driver—looking safe and highly dependable, judging by his proper conduct—had been quiet and studious at the wheels. Occasionally, he dipped low in the rear-view mirror to study us furtively, and briefly. And then, his curious eyes went back to the wet road ahead. Yes, he had been quiet all the way. But now, as though to reassure us—Dedeli, and me—he decided to speak.

"We are good for time," he announced in a solemn manner and said no more as we slid under that ultimate tunnel. His gentle and accented voice drew us out of our momentary torpor. And somehow—though I monitored the time on my own—I felt relief at the piece of information he just supplied.

See, on a previous BBC duty trip, I had arrived too late for boarding, lamentably missing the outbound flight. It was quite an unpleasant experience. I certainly didn't like the disruption that had come with it. Ever since, I am so much tormented with the prospect of running into a repeat of the same; so much so that I never can properly relax through the traffic jams any day I am on my way to the airport. And now, upon hearing the reassuring voice of the fellow, a nice *chill* effect came over me. At least, if anything were to go wrong with this trip, it wouldn't be that I failed to make it on time for my flight.

It took the good fellow some five minutes of further patience, and of some further inching forth between cars, before he could signal and safely negotiate a pull-over at the taxi ranks.

And mindful as to avoid lingering here any longer than necessary—lingering with the effect of holding up fellow cabbies in an avoidably slower queue—he briskly stepped out from behind the wheels and two strides later, he opened the rear of the grey Toyota MPV and unloaded my luggage.

And before he drove off, he took one second to do some further *unloading*. This time, it was the *unloading* upon me of some deeply-held opinion of his.

"I normally don't say this, brother," he stated in perfect English, speaking fast in chopped-up sentences, his eyes darting about as though he were on the look-out for some very evil spies. "I normally stick to my own business. But you look like a good guy; you have a beautiful wife." Here, with a slight *up-and-down* movement of his chin, he pointed past my shoulder in the direction of Dedeli who stood at my height. "Don't get killed there repeating the shameless propaganda of Bush and Blair. You are smart, brother. And you know it—It's for the oil. *The fucking oil.* You must *report* the truth. And stay alive. You have a lovely wife who will be waiting."

I expected the *brother* to jack up this *brotherly* intensity he had on display; I expected him to take it further and pat me friendly on the shoulder or something. But he didn't. He rather quickly brought the whole thing to a close with this parting shot: "Now, you please don't report me to the car company. Technically, this talk about the war is *unprofessional* of me. I am not supposed to go personal with passengers. So, do me a favour: Keep our little chat between us—I quite like driving *you* BBC folks around. Apart from a couple of assholes, BBC staff always treat me with respect."

Having said that, and with his hand reaching for the door, and him biting his bottom lip as though in defiance, the cabbie seemed to have no interest in my response to his impromptu speech. And as I was about to tell him that a journalist who detested random small talks from strangers was in the wrong business, he directed two rapid nods at me and lowered himself into the driver's seat of the MPV. A second later, he was gone, his mind probably on to his next job already.

Dedeli might have agreed with the driver's unsolicited counsel. But I don't remember her saying anything. On the issue of what might happen to me in Iraq, my wife and I said as little as possible. On my safety, we spoke in the unspoken code of silence. We both believed in the power of prayer. And we both understood that prayer loses of its soothing magic when it was undertaken against any psychological backdrop of doubt and fear and tenseness. We understood the standing prerequisites for *answered prayers*. But did I ever tell the driver that I was going to the War?

By the time I crossed the cabs' lane on my way back to Dedeli, after striding to the other side to fetch a trolley for the luggage, I still could not recall having explicitly told the driver that I was *shipping* myself out to the war. He might have overheard us at some point during the drive. But we did little talking if any at all. We were in quiet consultation with our private thoughts.

Or perhaps, as a regular service provider for that authorised BBC vendor—the car company—he might have drawn some inference from the BBC equipment, which formed the bulk of my luggage, and which readily suggested that I was bound for a far-away spot. And where in the world right now was some action that could prompt a BBC journalist to pack up for Heathrow?

If anything, what the driver did by the way of his brazen admonishment was to remind me, although redundantly, that the divisive issue of the war was the biggest conversation that united the world at this moment. As for his concern about my safety, I felt grateful for it. But did I know, as he said, that this was all for *the bloody oil*?

For impartiality reasons, the BBC would have frowned upon my venting out a personal opinion on the matter.

But oil as the actual reason for the invasion of Iraq was certainly a widely-held view, one stridently articulated by those screaming anti-war banners— those seen at demonstrations all over Parliament Square in Westminster and elsewhere around the world. For me, the question really was, "How would I fairly reflect this sentiment when it is time to go on *air* from the place I am headed to?"

The question mattered little at this point. I realised that my live transmission was not until days away, and that I needed to keep going, to survive until then.

All the same, I was still grappling in my head with the very question when—as Dedeli loyally tagged along—I stepped in cue for the large revolving gate that guarded the entrance to Terminal 4. Smooth and with no halting break, the gate leisurely spun around. And now taken in the uninterrupted cycle of this machine, we advanced obediently, all in step with the nonchalant speed of the thing.

Soon enough, the steel structure completed its rotation, delivering us with great mechanic indifference into the outer confine of the massive building. Here, immediately in the cool, light-flooded space, I took in the pleasant welcome of a faint and familiar scent—*The Scent of Heathrow*. It was unique, unmistakable, almost odourless. The Scent of Heathrow was hard to portray.

I can only say that it often spoke of places unknown, but ones that were not to remain so for long. On previous occasions—on my way to *maiden destinations*—the *Scent of Heathrow* played out as the evidence of impending discoveries, foreshadowing the demise of legends, of lies and of long-cherished myths.

And come to think of it now, it reminded me that I was on the cusp of my first trip ever to the Middle East. And under the known circumstances—the brutal uncertainty of war—I was now thinking of Heathrow as I never *ever* did before.

THE FATE OF the doomed *Titanic*—the ocean liner that sank in the Atlantic in 1912—told a story of more than a tragedy. Remember: More than 2,200 passengers were aboard the *unsinkable* ship when it went down under the frigid waters. That was quite a lot.

But *The Titanic*, with all its record-breakers, was just the tip of an iceberg—a loud note in a very eloquent speech that was a tribute to a mighty seafaring civilisation.

As a break-away *island* from continental Europe, Britain had always been a gift of the seas. A raw gift that had to be tamed, to be polished. Fortunately, the taming and the polishing were no problem: Britain was home to a *maritime genius*, hatched and groomed and later perfected in the cauldron of the Industrial Revolution. Thus, the seas that had given birth to it subsequently beheld as it went on to conquer them all. And thus, a true naval powerhouse saw the light of day.

Now, was that mastery of the seaways marshalled only for the sake of *sandbagging* warring rivals like the France of Napoleon Bonaparte? Was it just for the sake of pursuing further conquests in the service of an insatiable desire that demanded, ever and again, the subjugation of far-flung corners of the World?

Surely, there were strong elements of that. But beyond *territorial ambitions* and military considerations, the seaways were how Britain connected to the world for other peaceful, friendly, and commercial purposes, such as trade and travel. The seaways, of course, were how cargos of goods were lagged around early on; they were how passengers from *the nations* travelled to and from Britain.

Yes, the Island was both a primary destination and a stopover for passengers. It was the final or first port of call for the American bound for England, bound for Europe and for the wide world that lay beyond. And to most Europeans returning home, Britain was where they drew in the first breath of air that was truly a herald of home.

In those halcyon days of the ocean liners, the Port of London, with Tilbury at its heart—riding far ahead of Liverpool, Immingham, Southampton,

Hartlepool, Dover—was the busiest passenger port in the world, considering that London had long been a port even before it took over from Winchester and became the capital.

But somewhere between the beginning of World War II and the height of the Cold War that ensued, the history of passengers and how they travelled around the world came to a crucial junction; a junction where it was all set for a new fascinating chapter. And within a relatively short period of time, Heathrow would rise out of inexistence to become part of the world's collective memory. But how so?

Well, before motor-powered aircrafts became a banal utility for the purposes of warfare and for the business of flying passengers around, considerable time for trial and error *did have* to elapse, starting from when the Wright Brothers successfully flew the World's first airplane. As with most of the greatest inventions of Humanity, aviation exclusively was at first a military affair. In fact, the two World Wars would come along as a catalyst for the aviation industry. And by 1947—after the defeat of Hitler's Germany—the World's first commercial jet airliner, the *DH Comet,* rolled out of a factory in Britain.

The *Comet* was an engineering feat that announced a new area in the evolution of civil aviation. From the moment it took to the air in 1952, things rather had begun to *fly* at breakneck speed. The next two decades would usher in the Age of the Jumbo Jet, and the

Boeing 747—along with that European phenomenon named *The Concord*—would rule over the skies; they would be the superstars of the period.

By then, most of international travel has long shifted from the seaways to the skies. And by then, Heathrow was the world's busiest international airport.

Today, more than 67 million passengers travel through Heathrow every year; Heathrow that has since grown and expanded into a mega structure, with its five state-of-the-art terminals.

Today, Heathrow is the trading post for 90 airlines. Aircrafts speeding off from its runways fly away to more than 180 destinations in more than 90 countries. But just like commercial aviation itself, Heathrow's rise to prominence had been tentative, patient, gradual.

Back in 1930, sixteen years before the *Starlight*—that converted Lancaster bomber—became the first aircraft to take off from Heathrow on its way to Buenos Aires, the British aero engineer Richard Fairey caught sight of a conveniently-located plot of land at fourteen miles west of the embankment in Central London. The engineer, who was notable for the building and testing of aircrafts, decided to act on a luminous hunch and bought the 150-acres for £15,000, quite a fortune at the time. He marked no further delay in turning his handsome acquisition into a private aerodrome—the Fairey's Great West Aerodrome. From there, Richard would assemble and test his labour fruits. All was well for the aero engineer until the start of World

War II—in fact, until 1944 when the War entered its crucial year. In urgent need for a base to operate military aircrafts to carry combat troops to the Far East, the Government took hold of all the land that lay *in and around* the ancient agricultural village of Heath Row—the village that would later bequeath its name to the future modern airport.

As it happened, the designated land included Fairey's private aerodrome. And so, if the engineer were at a loss as to how he might contribute to the war effort, he was given a unique opportunity.

In any event, the Government lost no time in tearing things down in Heath Row village as it went ahead with the construction of the runways. Before long, the RAF Heston Aerodrome was up and running.

Then, a year after the fall of Nazi Berlin under the sustained fire of Soviet troops, the Government found itself with no further need of shipping servicemen to the Far East. The war was over. And RAF Heston had well and truly served its purpose. Now, it had to change hands.

And it did, with the army handing it over to the *Air Ministry*. Heston then began a new life: It became the new civil airport of London; it became the future Heathrow Airport, which is today—as noted earlier—the world's busiest international airport.

THESE MANY YEARS after World War II; these many years after Heathrow became a jewel in the crown of international civil aviation, Britain was once again busy in combat—this time, far from the home turf. Under *Operation Telic*, the Nation had committed as many troops to the front in Iraq as never before since World War II.

Of course, I didn't expect Heathrow to have somehow reverted to its military use of the past. Oh, yes—this Tuesday of April, I did not expect to see columns of British army personnel goose-stepping down the planks of *Terminal 4* in a roll-call manoeuvre before taking off for Basra.

The bulk of the service personnel, as committed to *Operation Telic*, had been in the combat zone since the first days of the war. But for reasons that were mainly political—the legal high hurdles Tony Blair had to clear before it was a go—the British troops had moved, with a great delay, into the theatre of operations, arriving there badly prepared and rather terribly equipped for the terrain and the risks. At any rate, any remaining soldiers would be rallying the front from the British Army outposts in the Gulf states, not from the main island; certainly not departing from Heathrow.

The only reason why my mind toyed with visualisation of the *Squaddies* was that I could think of nothing else right now. In fact, I would have taken the unexpected sight of men in military fatigues as a comfort. Comfort that I would not be flying out alone. But that was sure out of the question. In sight, I could see no men in fatigues. And that was fine. For this was Heathrow Airport. A civilian airport. Still, this Tuesday, Heathrow—at least, *Terminal 4*—looked none of what it usually did. Why? How? The concourse was almost empty. Passengers with trolleys in front or with luggage on wheels trailing behind appeared to be few and far apart. One could make a dash across the slick concourse without any significant obstruction. More alarmingly, the usually interminable queues at the baggage check-in stations were nowhere at sight. *Where are you, people?* I wondered.

For a moment, I indulged in the speculation that this might be part of the World's response to Britain's participation in the war. Yes, the anti-war protests, around the world and in London, were unabated. Brian Haw—the perfect living symbol of the popular revulsion at the invasion of Iraq—had by now been occupying Parliament Square for weeks. But could there be that the globetrotters of the world had also been protesting in a different manner, having chosen to stay away from Heathrow?

No, I was perhaps seeing everything through the *lens* of the war. Perhaps, even in time of peace, there were days like this around the year when passengers flocking through Heathrow dropped to a trickle. But of the countless times I had been here—whether in winter, spring, summer, or autumn—I had never seen Heathrow as sparsely attended as it was now.

BEFORE I SETTLED down reading that much into the *unusually* empty concourse, the good people of the *Royal Jordanian Airlines* had welcomed me for the handling of my luggage. The process was rather a *sail-through*, without even the slightest snag. I was travelling *heavy*, and Martina Wolf—the Office Manager who was always key in the successful planning of our duty trips—did the booking accordingly. She had taken care to pick a package that came with a preferential treatment, complete with a pre-emptive coverage of any excess luggage fees, with the highest end as a benchmark.

With *British Airways*, the BBC had a standing arrangement. This was meant to avoid any adverse scenario where excess luggage fees would become an issue. But this Tuesday, I was not travelling with *British Airways*. *Flight 112* to Amman was operated by the *Royal Jordanian Airlines*. And with no standing arrangement with the Jordanians, Martina spent a great deal of time customising my ticket. And I was glad she did: My emotions would be better spent where it mattered most—on the actual intricacies of reporting from the edges of danger.

At around 16:00, the long-awaited announcement rang over the Tannoy. *Flight 112* of the *Royal Jordanian Airlines* was now boarding. The patient voice of the lady on the speakers prayed that we proceed to the boarding gate.

I had by now hugged my wife and gone through

security. Suddenly, the Middle East—this region of the world we all think we know very well—was no longer just a name associated with trouble, somewhere far away from home. Suddenly, the Iraq War that had entered another phase took the aspects of a far greater tragedy than I could imagine so far. Now, I lowered my head and prayed. A familiar prayer:

The Lord is my shepherd; I shall not want.
He maketh me to lie down in green pastures:
He leadeth me beside the still waters.

He restoreth my soul: he leadeth
me in the paths
Of righteousness for his name's sake.
Yea, though I walk through the valley of the
shadow of death,

I will fear no evil: for thou art with me;
Thy rod and thy staff they comfort me.
Thou preparest a table before me in the pres-
ence of mine enemies:

Thou anointest my head with oil;
my cup runneth over.
Surely goodness and mercy
shall follow me all the days of my life:
And I will dwell in the house of
the Lord for ever.

This prayer, I would repeat at take-off. I would repeat it whenever I needed to return my mind to serenity. But for now, my thoughts went to my wife and the girls. They would be looking at the clock. They would know when exactly to virtually join me in the next *prayer session*. And as I thought about them, I *felt* them doing the same about me. To pray and always strive to see hope, that is a tradition. My family's tradition.

"Isaro just called to check the time the plane *actually* departs," my wife had told me, just moments after we bade farewell, and I left the concourse. I had chuckled at the tenderness of the whole thing and given her the precision she requested. Then, once again, I tasked her with reporting my *love* to the girls. I missed them already. And my thoughts would stay with them. Yes, until I was airborne. And throughout the flight.

At 16:55, the *Airbus 310* wheeled its nose under the patter of rain and rolled down the runway. Soon, it picked up speed, steadily climbed up, and ascended into the heavens. All the way... well, I prayed. And I knew Dedeli, Isaro and Astrida prayed too. Then— like a pilgrim—I gave a tacit chant, unheard by none:

The Land Between Two Rivers
Mesopotamia, here I come.
Iraq, yesterday of the Caliphate,
You are today at war, but I come in peace.
Keep me safe—I must go back home.

PART II

PASSAGE TO BAGHDAD

It seemed sensible to crave safety, to crave shelter from the bombs and the Birds and the daily depravity of war. But somewhere deep in her mind an idea had begun to fester—perhaps the longing for safety was itself just another kind of violence; a violence of coward-ice, silence, submission.

—OMAR EL AKKAD
American War

Chapter 11

IDLE HANDS IN AMMAN

Dedeli already wanted me back home. But she knew how ludicrous that was. How could she even think of my return now to Thamesmead, when I was still painstakingly on my way out? Realising that obtaining what she wanted was unreasonable, the girls' mother settled for an alternative, which was equally ludicrous: She resolved to fervently despise every additional day I spent in Amman, the Jordanian capital.

She had even come to detest the sound of it. I tried hopelessly to ease her troubled sentiments, explaining to her that *Amman* meant *safety* in Arabic. My point was that she shouldn't be so distressed over a name that had such a reassuring meaning. Of course, I was being creative with my explanation—my Arabic wasn't quite up to scratch.

As I had gathered from my poor compilation of key words and phrases, the actual Arabic word for safety is *amaan*. It was, however, close enough for my purposes, but it didn't work.

Dedeli still wanted me to move on. As far as she was concerned, progressing away from Amman and towards Baghdad—no matter how counterintuitive it seemed—would bring me closer to London. She knew it: There would be no return home before I had been to Baghdad and completed whatever task she believed needed to be done.

"How much longer will you be stranded there?" Dedeli asked over the phone, doing a good job of disguising her exasperation.

It was close to midnight here, bedtime in London. We had been speaking for a quarter of an hour. That was part of our nightly routine, a way for us to stay connected and keep up with each other's lives.

Stranded.

She didn't actually use the word *stranded*. She spoke in Kinyarwanda. Admittedly, French kept intruding, as it usually did. But for the most part, our conversation was in Kinyarwanda. As a rule of thumb, when there was no specific reason to use French or English, Kinyarwanda was our default language of communication. Not just because Rwandans, unlike many West Africans I knew, proudly held onto their language even after being away from home for many years.

Not just that.

It was also how we ensured that our language was passed on to the girls. Passing on the language was a crucial parental duty. Without Kinyarwanda, Isaro and Astrida—typical British middle-class school kids—would have been deprived of their Rwandan heritage. To me, that would be a form of psychological child abuse, with delayed effects. Thankfully, we did everything so we would never have to plead guilty to such an avoidable transgression.

Anyway, Dedeli's exact word—as spoken in Kinyarwanda—was not *stranded*. No, that's rather my best translation of it. And what an abuse, on my part, of the English language to speak of being *stranded* at the InterContinental Hotel in Amman. No, misery is a big part of being stranded. By any stretch, I couldn't say I was miserable that my stay at the *InterContinental* was being indefinitely extended. And I truly mean it.

The luxury hotel—smack in the heart of the Jordanian capital—stood with a grand display of extravagant majesty, commanding one of the seven hills of the city. The establishment provided convenient access to renowned attractions like the Roman Amphitheatre and the Citadel. Its rooftop, meticulously maintained, offered breath-taking views of the city skyline.

Ah, that rooftop.

For me, the rooftop served as a sanctuary for meditation and prayer. It held even greater significance after sunset than during the daytime. The experience of being on the rooftop played a substantial role in maintaining my calm resilience during our prolonged stopover in Amman. From that elevated vantage point, I would be captivated by the sight of the city's most iconic landmarks—the majestic King Abdullah I Mosque, the historic Rainbow Street, and the contemporary Abdali district. It made me feel as though I were closer to the heavens, closer to God.

Undoubtedly, the hotel had more to offer than just its awe-inspiring rooftop.

The complex, with its array of modern amenities, had a way of deceiving its guests into feeling as if they resided in a realm of wonders. While I never took advantage of the swimming pool and poolside areas, I made a habit of working up a sweat on the treadmills in the fitness centre. I also was a regular at the Atrium, one of the several restaurants within the InterContinental, where I indulged in delectable Lebanese lamb skewers and generous portions of authentic Italian pizzas.

I must emphasise that the food served at the Atrium—and forgive me for any exaggeration—was ambrosia. My goodness, the taste of the pizza still lingers in my memory; a delightful explosion of flavours that tantalised the buds, and which was yet gentle enough not to upset the stomach. An upset stomach would be a curse for anyone away from home, especially when embarking on a mission like the one I had at hand. In fact, though I was tempted by the fancier stuff on the menu, I opted for the safer choices. And thank *Allah*—should I say—the pizza served at the Atrium consistently did well by me. And that brings me to my point: It was difficult to feel stranded and miserable at the InterContinental.

"I'm not having a terrible time here," I sincerely reassured Dedeli, hoping that my response would suffice. "One day, sooner or later, after all of this is over, I'll bring you and the kids here for a holiday. You'll absolutely love it."

Dedeli scoffed, "How would a Christian woman like myself enjoy these places?"

These places? Oh, her words had come out with a hiss, and it made me cringe. It sounded too clichéd.

But no, I genuinely liked this place. The people I had encountered knew nothing of the coldness of ignoring strangers. They might not greet you with the customary *assalaamu alaikum*. Especially if they thought you were a black marine. But they wouldn't pass you by without acknowledging your presence. And there was something strangely captivating about the ubiquitous call to prayer. It was unique, and I knew I would miss it when I eventually left the city.

"It doesn't matter," I challenged Dedeli, "as a Christian, you will experience Amman in a different way. But it can still be pleasant."

My wife remained unconvinced. "I can't see myself enjoying wearing a headscarf."

"Come on," I urged. "It's Amman, not Mecca. It's Jordan, not Saudi Arabia."

Choosing to remain sour, my wife seemed determined not to be swayed. "Not Mecca?" she responded sceptically. "Well, I'd still have to adhere to some dress code there, right?"

I had to agree with her that she would still have to dress modestly. "But Dedeli," I said, "since when has dressing modestly been a problem for Africans? Let's be careful not to condescend to others—Arabs or anyone else."

"What does that even mean?" she replied, clearly irritated.

I pictured furrows forming on her delicate forehead. Those furrows were a tell-tale sign of her irritation. She was rarely irritated, but when she was, those furrows appeared.

"This is what I mean," I explained, "We live in Britain, but if you do come to Amman, you must have the sense to respect the locals and their culture. When in Rome—"

"—do as the Romans do," the girls' mother interjected, her tone bitter, before falling silent. Her sudden silence troubled me within mere seconds.

"Don't get me wrong," I said, trying to salvage our conversation. "Rwandans are not known for bashing other cultures. There's something colonial about having a narrow-minded perspective on culture. As Africans, we should know better."

As I continued speaking, I felt as if I were channelling that BBC Arabic producer—an inspiring hijab-wearing young Moroccan woman who cherished her life in Britain as much as she cherished her headscarf. The cloth, as she wore it, would frame her face in a serene and beautiful way.

I once stood by the rear portico of Bush House, listening attentively as she passionately defended her cultural attire. In her gentle accented English, she patiently argued that it takes a great deal of arrogance for anyone to suggest that their way of dressing is the universal standard. She believed it to be close-minded to think that the more we reveal, the more liberated we become.

"The freedom lies in the choice," the Moroccan woman declared to her attentive BBC colleagues. "Arabs, much to the chagrin of our narrow-minded friends, are not eager to disrobe. We don't yearn to dress in skimpy clothes. We desire the freedom to live in accordance with what pleases Allah. And I am tired of hearing privileged white women tell me how oppressed I am because I don't dress like they do. In Britain, the only oppression I feel is from the condescending gaze of those who want to liberate me from what I have freely chosen to wear."

Having now appropriated, recycled, and presented my colleague's argument, I felt that I had been overly intense with Dedeli. However, I hoped she now understood why we shouldn't make an issue out of how others choose to dress. But Dedeli remained determined to be sour tonight.

"You know what?" she scoffed sarcastically, "You sound like you should apply for a job with the *Saudi Arabia Broadcasting Corporation*. Do they hire Africans there?"

She might have intended it as a playful remark, but I wasn't amused. So, I replied, "Once again, Dedeli, I am in Jordan, not Saudi Arabia."

"They are neighbours," she blurted out. "And they are all in Arabia."

It all seemed out of character for my wife to be acting this way. I wondered what the real underlying issue could be. Was it anxiety? Did she have lingering fears about my safety here? Ironically, she had been quite calm about every step of my duty trip so far.

In a calm manner, I asked, "What are you not telling me, Dedeli?"

We were met with the same prolonged silence that had become all too familiar. Then, the girls' mother spoke up. "There's something I don't quite understand. You knew when you would arrive in Amman, but you don't know when you're leaving? It's been five days now, and counting."

Suddenly, it dawned on me that this conversation was not really about the subject being openly discussed. So, I responded, "Is that really what's troubling you?"

"Okay," Dedeli snapped, "tell me honestly: Are you with someone there?"

It was a surprise.

But I couldn't say I didn't understand. It was the resurfacing of that old witch—suspicion. Yes, theoretically, trust shouldn't eliminate the need for checks. The spouse who claims to be on a duty trip could potentially be using it as a cover for an affair. It's natural for loved ones to sometimes harbour such doubts. And if they are mistaken, it is our responsibility to dispel those doubts, those unfounded suspicions.

"Listen," I said calmly, "I love you."

"No," she protested sharply, "that's not what I want to hear. I assume you love me. I hope that hasn't changed."

Sadness welled up inside me. "Well," I sighed, "if you believe that to be true, if you believe that I love you, then I suppose that's all you need to hear."

"Venuste," Dedeli called, her usually warm voice now filled with coldness. Whenever she addressed me by my full name like that, I knew she was deadly serious. "I want a direct answer," she stated firmly, a statement that sounded more like a dire warning than anything else.

I took a breath to steady my nerves. "Okay, you're right," I said. "I am with more than just someone."

She cried out, "I knew it!"

"Let me finish," I pleaded. "Remember, we are a whole team from the BBC heading to Baghdad. Here in Amman, we gather for the rest of the journey. We won't depart until the last member of the team arrives in town. Even then, we won't set out until Security gives us the go-ahead. So, yes, I knew when I would arrive in Amman, but I can't tell you when we'll be heading out. And apparently, it's all for the sake of our safety."

After another silence, during which Dedeli must have been contemplating what I had just said, she cleared her throat and spoke to me with great affection, "I love you. And I know that you love me too. You always have. For that, I thank you. And thank you forever for our beautiful girls. They miss you so much. We want you back home safe."

The return of tenderness in Dedeli's voice as she expressed her love and concern for me choked me up. It was curious how affection and grief could manifest in the same way, with a tightness in the chest and tears welling up in the eyes.

Sniffing and trying to regain composure, I replied, "I miss you too, all of you. And of course, I'll be back home. That's what God has decreed. With your love and the love of our children, I will always remain resilient."

We spoke some more, renewing various promises to each other. And just before Dedeli hung up, she offered some advice. "While you wait there in the beautiful city of Amman, don't be idle." There was a significant pause. "Idle hands are the devil's workshop."

Dedeli was ever that Bible-quoting Christian girl. I couldn't complain about that. Now, I certainly wasn't idle at all.

I was documenting every aspect of my duty trip, including this prolonged stopover. I found great value in reviewing the details of the backstory and the key players in the war. It provided perspective when reporting on subsequent developments in the conflict. Accurately capturing the details required a lot of research and study. So, I couldn't afford to be idle even if I wanted to.

Perhaps what Dedeli meant was that she needed to hear me on the BBC, filing reports regularly like special envoys do. Hearing my voice on the BBC, along with our nightly catch-ups, would reassure her doubly that everything was truly well.

Coincidentally, there were a few colleagues back at Bush House who shared Dedeli's *idle-hands* concerns, but for entirely different and cynical reasons. According to them, I was enjoying myself, having the time of my life, running around the luxurious InterContinental hotel while I should have already been making appearances on various studio programs through satellite phone, enhancing the BBC's coverage of the war, regardless of whether I had reached Baghdad or not.

Such criticism didn't necessarily have to be fair. In our line of work, the official stance was that cooperation was paramount. However, in the minds of many colleagues, the notion of competition—for professional respect and future promotions—never took a leave. Sniping at perceived competitors wasn't uncommon.

And sometimes, the unpleasant prodding of gossiping lips was needed to bring out our best, to push through what we thought was impossible, and to accelerate what we intended to delay. Adversity is often underestimated—it can serve as a powerful fuel. "Thanks, Dedeli," I told my wife. "I won't be idle."

BEFORE I DISAPPEARED amidst the plush white bedsheets of the InterContinental for the remainder of the short night, I retrieved my small notebook of prayers. Opening it to a random page, I focused my attention and, in whispered tones, read a psalm to myself, gathering my spirits and finding solace in the words.

Chapter 12

A CASE OF LIMITED CREDENTIALS

I sat with BBC Field Team Leader *Richard Blunt* at a table in the *Atrium* that soared up to a glass dome, which would open onto the Jordanian sky. In this lively setting by the hotel's lobby, we indulged in green olives and sipped on tamarin cocktails, discussing the upcoming trek to Baghdad.

Richard was an imposing figure with a neatly trimmed head of black hair that accentuated his round mouth. His English carried a strong and harsh accent, which initially posed a challenge for my Rwandan ears. While he was a native English speaker from London, his raw accent would leave a significant portion of the audience perplexed if he were to read the news in it. It was rare to hear anyone at the BBC speaking with such a perplexing accent; people at BBC business meetings knew when to instinctively switch to what I was first introduced to as BBC English.

English.

One thing I quickly discovered was that the notion of an *English* or *British* accent was a myth. There was no single accent that could be attributed to all English or British speakers. There were nearly as many *English* or *British* accents as there were post codes. And that was perfectly fine. What seemed absurd, however, was the occasional anger of radical class warriors who believed that anyone from outside the United Kingdom, given a choice, would have gone to school and learned to speak a specific regional dialect. For every language in the world, there existed a standard business version understood by the majority of speakers, both natives and otherwise. Naturally, that standard version was what any learner, who was responsible and invested their time and effort wisely, would strive to acquire. It was a matter of practicality and economics.

No, I was always adamant not to be dragged into certain whimsical aspects of the class warfare—this thing that was as much British as fish and chips. And on that account, I put little patience in my dealings with any ideologue who believed that everyone owed them a duty of familiarity with their *post-code* accent. The truth was, that *post-code slang* would be of little use in helping a black man secure a decent job—not with the BBC anyway. And Richard knew that. So, did he expect me to suddenly be familiar with his vernacular?

Not really.

In certain circles, some of the Queen's subjects would resort to using an impenetrable argot when they felt irritated by one's comfort around them. It was a subtle reminder that, regardless of how well you thought you were assimilated, you would never truly belong. But let there be no confusion. Although I had sworn allegiance to the Queen and am grateful to be a British citizen—at a visceral and instinctive level—I am *Rwandan.*

Therefore, any attempt to put me in my place, through the *post-code* games, would fall flat. You can't put someone in their place when they already inhabit that place.

At any rate, Richard Blunt knew that, if he intended to be understood by me, or by our Jordanian hosts for that matter, he had to knock out that hermetic slang of his; Richard Blunt understood that discussing BBC business with me in his own vernacular would be akin to showing up at work in one's underpants—amusing, but unfitting and potentially indecent.

In a light-hearted yet serious manner, I protested, intending it as a joke. "Could you turn off your post-code accent, please? This is official BBC business, sir!"

"Sorry about that," Richard replied with a prolonged chuckle. "I suppose I wouldn't fare well if you spoke to me in Nigerian Pidgin, would I?"

No, I didn't speak Nigerian Pidgin. But I was glad Richard got the point.

"Not a big deal," I said. "But I thought we could work more efficiently if I didn't have to constantly guess what's coming out of your mouth."

Richard found my comment amusing and laughed heartily. And after he calmed down, I asked him, "What did the security specialists say? Can I file dispatches from here? Your answer better be yes—some of my teammates in London are pretty pissed."

Richard's big grey eyes widened. "What in the world are they pissed about?"

"They think it's outrageous that I'm stranded in this incredibly luxurious hotel, enjoying food and drinks at the expense of the British taxpayer, while remaining silent about the war. They want me to file on just about anything. As long as they can say it's from their special envoy in the Middle East, they can rest."

Richard patted me on the shoulder. "Why don't you tell the bastards to take a seat for a moment!?" he said, and added immediately: "Well, that was a joke. Strike it. But if you want, you can tell them to back off. Why can't we file when we're ready, and when it's appropriate and meaningful to do so?"

I shook my head slightly and looked directly at Richard's well-groomed facial hair. "That's thoughtful advice, and I appreciate you sharing it. But I'm inclined to indulge those bastards if there's a way. Now, what are the concerns of the security team? What do they advise?"

The atmosphere shifted as Richard's demeanour

turned serious. He kept his hard post-code accent repressed, almost as if it had never existed, and he began to explain the situation. "Technically," he said, "Jordan is a friendly country, a Western-friendly country. However, if you want to leave this hotel and venture outside for reporting, you'll need more than just a transit visa. Without proper credentials, there's a real risk of getting arrested. We don't want that. And Security is concerned about more than just your limited admin leeway."

His response left me puzzled still. "What else is there to be concerned about?" I asked.

Richard said gravely, "Well, your safety."

His answer didn't bring me closer to the clarity I sought. "Come on," I said. "Are you suggesting that Jordan is more dangerous than Baghdad, where we are headed?".

"Certainly, that's not what Security says."

I shifted anxiously, disappointed in myself for potentially overlooking a security risk in my assessment of Amman. "How does Security see it?" I asked.

"Jordan is not Iraq," Richard explained, "but the shadow of the war hangs over this place. There's an element of the war present here. That makes it dangerous in an unpredictable way. Danger often lurks where and when it's least expected. When you're not anticipating trouble, you may not be in the right mindset to remain vigilant. And that can be deadly. It's a serious concern for the security team."

As Richard spoke on, the full picture began to emerge. Amman may not have been Baghdad, but there was a strong sentiment of solidarity across Jordan. The invasion of Iraq was perceived as an attack on all Arabs and Muslims, and this sentiment reverberated throughout the entire Middle East.

Now, if you were in town, wielding a press microphone with a BBC flag on it, quietly advertising yourself as someone from the other leading country of the Coalition, you didn't want to run into the wrong type of vengeful crowd that might be seeking to exact retaliation of some kind. Perhaps, in the name of Allah, or for whatever wound the assault on Saddam might have inflicted on the collective *Umma*. The irony was that Saddam, the liquor-sipping megalomaniac who gassed Kurds, seemed to have little regard for the Umma. The Umma was merely a convenient rallying cry when the Americans came shooting.

At any rate, the security team had a valid point. Being kidnapped or killed in Baghdad would be horrendous, but falling victim to such a fate in Amman due to overconfidence and a false sense of safety would be both terrible and foolish.

I took a moment to process the situation and then turned to Richard, half-heartedly conceding that my options might be limited. "So, what is the advisory?" I asked. "Should I simply tell the team in London to back off?"

Above the neat tapestry of cropped hair, Richard

licked his bottom lip, as he looked at me with a vivid grin, his eyes sparkling with amusement. "It would be absolutely fantastic if you told them to back the hell off," he chuckled. "But I understand that's not what you want to do."

"No, it's not," I affirmed.

"In that case," Richard said, rising to his feet, "I suppose you can offer them a compromise: two-ways, but strictly from within the confines of the hotel. You can either do it from your room or from the rooftop. As for the subjects you cover, that will be up to you."

"I'm open to suggestions," I said eagerly.

"Yes, you are," Richard noted. "You can gather a lot from the local papers available at the Reception desk. Of course, the internet is always at your disposal. Reuters is a reliable source for the usual types of things—background information, profiles, and so on. Now, remember: You don't have the necessary credentials or security clearance to venture out there and engage in on-the-ground reporting. File or don't. But don't go out there."

Richard gave me a gentle pat on the arm, quickly downed his tall glass of tamarin cocktail, and walked away, leaving me to ponder the critical need to balance safety and newsgathering.

RATHER DISPIRITED, I felt this balancing act between safety and newsgathering was a disappointing compromise; one that shed new light on the old cliché,

Truth is the first casualty of war. How could we salvage the truth from the wreckage of war when we have to keep a safe distance to avoid arrest or death?

For the first time, faced with this reality, beyond all the armchair theories, I stared at the sobering limits of my role as a special correspondent out here. I was sure to have uncovered one of the biggest lies about war reporting—the shameless presentation of what ultimately aired as the definitive truth about war. No, the war stories that end up in the media are more like decent sketches of the truth than the whole truth.

Chapter 13

FOR OLD TIME'S SAKE

Altogether, studio manager *Neil Watson* had about a dozen tattoos on various parts of his body, but Neil still had plans to go under the needle sometime in the future. Perhaps, after this duty trip. For sure, Neil had not been definitive on his timing for an eventual return to the tattoo parlour. And I didn't press him on it.

"Thanks for coming," I said, holding the door ajar to admit Neil to the balcony of my hotel room, where the BGAN satellite kit already awaited. I thought about getting the affable Neil into *the zone* with a calculated instant booster—a chat about his beloved tattoos. But I considered that priority should go to the business. So, I said: "It's a pre-recorded two-way. We should be connected to Bush House *Studio C*, where the presenter will be waiting. He must now have started his night shift. And *Control Room* expects us in a little over an hour's time."

"An hour? That's plenty of time," Neil said, cheerfully. Then, turning around to look at me quizzically, he went on: "Why in the name of Jesus Christ would you pre-record what can be done live? *Yours truly* is yours full-time. I can wake up as early as you wish, just to set you up. You only need to instruct me and just watch."

"My dear Neil," I scoffed, "but you are forgetting something?"

Neil took a step forward, reaching for the pieces of hardware on the tabletop. "Enlighten me, please."

"By the time the show is on-air," I said, "it would be 8:30 a.m. here. I think we would have long crossed the border into Saudi Arabia. You didn't get the memo?"

"Bloody me!" Neil patted his forehead with an open palm, in a gesture of sudden realisation. I forgot indeed that we're soldiering on tomorrow! But yes, I did get the memo."

"You know," I said, "there's a reason why we forget things."

"Yes, it's psychology," Neil observed, unpacking the BGAN kit. "I guess that, at a subconscious level, I don't want to leave Amman." Something in how that came out struck a sorrowful note. "It's been just under a week," Neil continued. "But it's hard to say goodbye to the InterContinental."

"Word," I said.

"Well, lemme get down to work." That was delivered with an imperceptible sigh. And with that, Neil got down to work. Soon, he called *Control Room* and tested the line.

Perfect.

And the very personable Neil looked buoyant over the outcome. And I could relate.

With our protracted stopover, he had begun to itch for action. This little job tonight wasn't much, of course. But it came as a promise that he would soon be properly busy as he should. And that was great. As for now, though, Neil was poised to step back out, and return in time to redial the *Control Room*, to put me in touch with presenter *Michel Christophe*.

But before he could retreat, I decided to grant him a little treat he would enjoy—the delayed tattoo talk.

"How many have you got?" I asked, pointing at the *steeple* decoration on his naked right bicep. "It is so beautiful!"

Neil beamed. "I got twelve. Or maybe, fifteen!?" He laughed, appearing genuinely overjoyed, genuinely happy. "Well, I'm really not counting any more. At least, not since I inked my tenth."

Provocatively, I asked, "And when are you getting one somewhere on the face?"

"On my face?" Neil looked up at me as though I really had no clue whatsoever about tattoos. Then, he said firmly: "*Never*. I mean, a tattoo! It literally should never get in anybody's face." He laughed at his own double entendre. "Anywhere below the neck, that's fine. But when it starts creeping higher past that point, then you start looking like a creep. And that will never be me."

I nodded. "That's good to know."

"What's going on, here?" Something unexpected lit up on Neil's beardless white face. "Are you considering going under the needle yourself?" And saying that, the studio manager grinned broadly, as though he was happy at the prospect of someone new joining the club.

"Not at all," I said.

The engineer looked disappointed. "Why not?"

I hesitated before saying cheekily, "The black body isn't your ideal canvas for tattoos."

Here, I couldn't help but consider the seemingly perpetual pale skin of Neil Watson. Almost a week in sunny Jordan clearly had done little to work a tan into him.

"There are things that work better on our black bodies," I continued. "But even the best tattoo would fail to stand out in all its wondrous details on a typically African ebony skin."

I am not typically ebony. But I was just feeding an argument, to mess a bit with my pal. And I got him.

"Listen," Neil prayed, after freezing for a moment, lost for a word, then declaring at last, with a repressed laugh: "I didn't say that. Are we clear?"

"No, we are not," I teased. "You said it."

"You are very cheeky, Venuste," Neil observed. "But if you are logging a memo about this conversation, let it reflect that I said no such thing about black bodies and tattoos. Not my area of expertise." He laughed some more.

Then, he stepped off the balcony into the room and headed for the door.

"See you in a bit," he said over his shoulder and disappeared by the time the door latch travelled back up.

Taking seat at the transparent glass desk, where I would review the scripted draft of my impending two-way, I muttered, *"Funny guy?"* And for the next moment, I flashed back to the first time I was paired with Neil Watson for a BBC duty trip.

OUT IN THE field, the pressure of transmission deadlines could sometimes make a complete jerk of an otherwise perfectly reasonable human being. But then, one could fortunately learn a useful lesson; for example, the lesson that being a jerk was not dignifying. Anyway, I once made a complete jerk of myself; I once shouted at that BBC studio manager—one Neil Watson—who had been assigned to me for a duty trip to Mali, where our remit was to cover a presidential election.

The incident occurred over an evening in the last 24 hours of our stay. At five minutes to airtime—with me slotted in pole position to beam live into the studio from a polling station in Bamako—Neil was yet to route the satellite link through to the *Control Room* at Bush House. Let's say he thus brought about the kind of situation that didn't promote good cardiac health. Yes, the sense that I was about to let down the team in London elicited a very foul feeling in me; it had left me racked with two variants of the same grief.

First, there was the concern that I was about to blow a decent scoop.

And what was it?

The chairman of the local electoral commission had just told me, in an exclusive interview, that former Army Officer Amadou Toumani Touré, who once unhooked Mali from the grip of a dictator, was headed for a big electoral win. If I missed the 6:00 p.m. slot, the scoop—thus delivered on a silver platter—would forever lose its value as such.

And this was how the matter stood: *BBC French* would not be back on air before the next transmission the following morning at 4:30 a.m. By then, Radio France International—the direct competitor of *BBC French* across Africa—would have ruthlessly depleted the story of all its freshness. I did not appreciate that prospect. To sit on a scoop, however minor, only to get round to it when it had become a stale piece of cold news!?

That was depressing.

My second concern was about something more disconcerting, still.

The live set-up from the polling station was meant

to be the crowning show of our whole assignment. We had done a good job so far, going long days without food, sitting up most nights till late, editing packages that were then *FTPed* to London. Long hours, going hungry on the job—that came with the territory. So, the whole experience was rather an honour.

But now, I stood to look like a foot, if I bungled this opportunity to report *timely* on the ultimate outcome of what had been an arduous process. And yet, there we were! Struggling to get through to the studio, where the output producer was probably throwing a magnificent fit.

As it happened, with plenty of time to spare, Neil had tested the BGAN satellite connection, without running into the slightest snag. But now that we needed it for real, the line kept dropping, and a very stubborn vocal prompt kept patronising us: *"It has not been possible to establish a connection; hang up and try again."*

As the looming catastrophe played out, I bathed in a film of sweat amid the oppressive heat of the early evening, spacing around like a mad man, progressively losing my wits with every striking second.

Meanwhile, Neil Watson had kept it all together. With the focus of a bomb disposal technician working to defuse an explosive, he wouldn't be distracted either by my fretting or by that inexorable countdown to airtime. And his vivid unfazed demeanour—rather than calming me down—did the opposite.

Yes, I was fazed by his placidity.

Ultimately, I blew a fuse and yelled, "Why the hell could you not have left the connection up and running!? This is unacceptable sabotage. You knew that getting the line back up and ready here wouldn't be a piece of cake—We are in Bamako, not in Bayswater!"

Neil just shot a seemingly murderous glance at me, probably wondering what the hell *Bayswater* got to do with this. But he stoically refused to be distracted.

To him clearly, it was ridiculous, the notion that he should have left the satellite link all up, with the risk of running one of the highest telecommunication bills ever incurred by a BBC team for such a single short transmission. Neil's cold, fleeting gaze suggested a belief that a screw must have got loose in my head. But no, it was just the stress.

Immediately, in the face of Neil's imperturbability, I regretted my little tantrum. Yes, if not because it was outright wrong, at least it looked absolutely weird that I should be shouting at the only White man in this very black African neighbourhood. To the onlookers, it definitely seemed like an ugly petty scene of some black vengeance. I was disgusted by it. And seething regretfully, I said, "Sorry, Neil! I am very sorry!"

"It's all right, mate," Neil said. And almost right on cue, he pointed at the little mobile mixer on the foldable desk. "We are through, *sir*. Gather your shit together. Press down the red button and talk to the output studio manager."

I looked at the button, ashamed to a great deal.

"Sure, take your time but not too much," Neil said. "We've only got three minutes."

That evening in Bamako, the live broadcast went well. Once we were off-air, I wholeheartedly apologised to Neil Watson once again.

"That was a terrible move," I said, not mincing my words in my attempt to make amends.

Neil chuckled. "You're absolutely right. It was a major-league dick move."

Still in a repentant state and eager to continue making up for my actions, I offered, "If you're documenting this incident, please make sure it reflects that I behaved poorly. I mean it, completely."

"Can I tell you something?" Neil asked kindly.

"Sure, go ahead," I replied.

"For better or worse, I always stand by my teammates," he said, resonating with uncomplicated integrity. "I have no issue with the concept of bosses, but I don't need a boss to function properly. Look, we're both adults here. We can handle our own disagreements. And actually, that outburst?" He flashed me a thumbs-up. "It kept me determined, unwilling to give up. What it showed is that you take your job seriously—hardly a transgression that could justify a damning memo. Nonetheless, I want you to know something, Venuste."

"Tell me," I said.

"No matter how dire a live situation may seem, if

it's a technical issue, trust your technical guy and, for fuck's sake, give him a chance to fix it," Neil advised. "If it can't be fixed, all your huffing and puffing is utterly useless. If it can be fixed, you become a distraction by interfering with his focus."

I simply smiled. He was absolutely right.

Neil continued, "When the mic is open and you're doing your thing, do I feed you what you need to say?"

"No, you don't," I replied.

"Exactly," he said triumphantly, standing a foot away. "I don't even speak bloody French. How could I?"

I chuckled. "Shall I respond to that?"

"For God's sake, no. My point is, I don't handle your on-air delivery, so return the courtesy and stay away from the technical side of things. That's how we can be one hundred percent sure we won't drive each other to *murder* while we're out here on this bloody BBC assignment."

We laughed off the notion of driving each other to murder, and then we drove back to our hotel in time for dinner.

Since that incident in Bamako, both at Bush House and on other assignments, I had been paired with Neil Watson many times. I was glad that Neil was one of the field studio managers who had joined us in Amman for this duty trip to Baghdad.

Chapter 14

THE TROUBLE WITH ANTOINE

Some people—it's often said—can stab you in the back, and then turn around to complain that you made them sweat, because the planting of their bloody dagger between your shoulders was hard work. Well, producer *Antoine Édouard* reminded me of this toxic type. That's why I never lowered my guard around him.

"We started to despair that you'd ever file," Antoine said, when—at a long last—he crossed into the studio and picked the ISDN signal.

I said nothing and he went on. "You really think the BBC organised all of this, just to give you some holidays amidst the *Bedouins*?"

This was a masterclass in passive aggression.

And I was incommensurably needled by it.

With my Sony headphones screwed into place, and with my right fingers forming a hollow fist around the stem of the unidirectional microphone, I had sat alone on this balcony, waiting for someone to arrive and pick this damn call. I had been waiting since Neil—the studio manager—returned, connected me to *Control Room* and disappeared back into those corridors. I had rehearsed my script aloud, and got bored going through it three more times. Then, I had just sat, listening to the silent vacuum over the ether, my gaze vaguely plunging into the late night of Amman, with its lights spreading out beyond the hotel's parapets.

All in all, it had been more than ten minutes since the *Control Room* patched the connection through to *Studio* C. It had been this long!

And it was only now that Antoine Édouard brought himself along. And he was gutsy enough to attempt shrugging the whole thing off, by way of seeking to guilt-trip my *ass*.

I know it's unwise to pick a fight with a skunk, as one would still smell terrible even if one comes up on top. But I was willing to take my chances, here.

So, bating my breath, I told Antoine: "The word you should be looking for is *sorry*, Monsieur Édouard."

"Seriously!" The bastard chuckled. "*Sorry* for what?"

"What happened?" I asked him. "One single minute of BGAN uptime comes down to six Pounds Sterling. And every penny of it is recorded against the charge code of *BBC French*. By running a quick calculation, more than £100 just went up in thin air, simply because you needed to take your time to get into the studio there. I am not very enthusiastic about being tied up here, waiting for you. But I'm sure there must be a reason."

Antoine stalled, then sighed. "If the big British Broadcasting Corporation is this broke that £100 may break the bank," he sneered spitefully, "I suggest they close the goddamn thing down and auction it off to Rupert Murdoch."

That sounded about right. It was classic Antoine Édouard. Whenever cornered and pressed to take responsibility, he always managed to stage a righteous indignation of such a high order that it would overshadow any real wrong he might have done. Tonight at least, it wasn't all grief for me. I succeeded in cutting him off from that guilt-trip he had embarked upon.

"Listen, *bonhomme*," Antoine Édouard said, just when I was giving up any hope that he might apologise. "I don't care about this cold, soulless institution, and I would not apologise for costing it a few quids. Okay? But at a personal level, if you want me to apologise to you, why not?"

Now apparently unwrapping a new radio magnetic tape to fit into the clunky recording machine, Antoine—sounding far off the studio microphone—added: "By the way, you should remember to take care of yourself out there. You work yourself to death, that'd be on you. They'll replace you in the blink of an eye. These people don't give a rat's ass about either you or me."

A rat's ass. The bat of an anopheles' wings.

Antoine had a knack for using such unconventional phrases, and he had me laughing away my anger, which wasn't too bad. And as I laughed, I couldn't help but ponder what a peculiar character he was. Always slender with a youthful face, he seemed to have good genes, but his personality was far from healthy.

The man practically detested everything that moved on the newsroom floor. It wasn't just his dislike for his own fellow countrymen; I can't recall anything he hated more than the British. Tony Blair, in particular, irked him to no end. Frankly, I often wondered why someone so anti-British would choose to live in Britain, let alone work for the British Broadcasting Corporation.

Whatever may have gone wrong in Antoine's childhood remained a mystery. At least to me. He would have been a challenging case even for the esteemed Carl Jung himself. However, it was no mystery that he believed in a great destiny that perpetually eluded him. He often hinted at grand achievements in a past life before joining the BBC, but there was no evidence to support these claims of grandeur.

"You are a peculiar and deeply twisted individual, you sad sonofabitch," Broadcast Assistant Wendy had once tearfully told Antoine Édouard. "I do not wish you well."

Wendy had printed a private memo in which she

had expressed rather unpleasant thoughts about the editor. In her haste to catch her train at Euston Station, she forgot to collect the defamatory document from the printer's tray. When Antoine arrived for his night shift and stumbled upon the accidentally *declassified* note, he couldn't resist revelling in it.

To be clear, Antoine had no sympathy for the slandered editor. He simply relished the opportunity to make a hell of someone else's life.

And this is what he did: he meticulously photocopied the incriminating memo and ensured that a copy was placed in each of our pigeonholes. One by one, we returned to the office the next day and were confronted with the embarrassing revelation—Wendy's honest and unflattering opinion of her manager.

Fortunately, the editor chose to take the high road. He never made a fuss about the entire incident. And when a few colleagues pressed Antoine for an explanation of his sordid behaviour, he quite hypocritically provided one.

"There is something malicious and subtly dangerous about a colleague writing derogatory remarks against their boss," Antoine had argued, with a poker face. "If they are capable of doing that to the boss, they can do worse to you. So, I considered myself fortunate to witness something I cannot condone or support. I saw it as my moral duty to take action."

What truly motivated Antoine's actions remained a mystery. Some speculated about an unrequited office romance, but the truth was still out there. The Frenchman was fortunate that Wendy—perhaps, because of her own obvious guilt—didn't push for disciplinary measures.

Anyway, that was the kind of person who had kept me waiting on the satellite phone for over ten minutes and had attempted to deflect away from his dereliction by guilt-tripping me.

"Thank you, Antoine," I said after he finished his non-apology and offered his unsolicited advice. "I appreciate your concern, and I will certainly take care of myself. However, I would be more satisfied if you could provide me with the true reason for your delay. I'll be out here for weeks, and it could be helpful in mitigating issues the next time I'm calling the Control Room. What really happened? That's more practical than a personal apology."

First, there was a sigh of annoyance, followed by a reasonably plausible explanation.

"The Control Room alerted us that you were ready," Antoine offered. "But then I completely forgot about it. Unintentionally. I got caught up in reviewing a terribly edited tape." It was still unfortunate, but that explanation sounded genuine. Antoine had a reputation for being forgetful, and I suppose I was fortunate that he eventually remembered I was waiting.

"Where is the presenter?" I asked, swiftly shifting to the next pressing issue. "Or are you going to conduct the two-way yourself?"

"*Michel Christophe* called to inform us that he's running late," Antoine replied.

And seemingly realising that he was being too lenient towards the absent presenter, he added disdainfully, "The marsupial has started to believe he's a big star now, thinking he can decide when to start his shifts. I'm yet to see any evidence that we truly have a competent manager in charge."

I remained silent, refraining from contributing even a single word to the disparagement of the absent presenter. It was risky to participate in any way in Antoine's slanderous remarks. Rumours could soon circulate, suggesting that I had maliciously criticised a colleague. Antoine Édouard himself would be the first to mysteriously take offense at my dishonourable behaviour, the kind he claimed he would neither support nor encourage.

Bottom line is, Antoine was undeniably a deeply troubled individual.

"What's the plan, *Le Grand Édouard*?" I asked. He took great pleasure in being referred to as *Le Grand Édouard*—the Great Edward.

"Let's get this done," he proposed, "unless you'd rather do it live tomorrow, which I understand is out of the question. Let's proceed now!"

For the next five minutes, drawing on my harvest from raiding the columns of the local press and mining the news wires, I provided Antoine Édouard with my best possible account of how much the war next door was being felt here in Jordan. And of what I said about the influx of Iraqi refugees, the tightened security at the border, and the angry opposition from religious leaders, none appeared to arouse any personal sentiment in the Frenchman. Yet, Antoine became visibly incensed when I concluded the two-way with these remarks:

> *The official position here in Jordan is a delicate one: the Government of His Majesty is a Coalition ally. As a result, the country is home to a base of operations for U.S. and Coalition forces, which are granted permission to use the country's airspace; they share intelligence with the Coalition. Yet, Jordan—even as Baghdad has since fallen—is still formally opposed to regime change in Iraq. This self-contradiction in the official position is driving the anger, mainly of the Muslim Brotherhood, which is a perfectly legal movement here.*

"What a messed-up position that is!" Antoine exclaimed immediately after I finished my sign-off. "You're assisting the Americans in their actions against Saddam, while simultaneously claiming you don't want Saddam removed?"

The last I heard before the line cut off in a string of *beeps* was Antoine unleashing a curse in French.

"Le Roi Abdallah de Jordanie nous prend pour des nez percés, ou quoi?" he fumed. *"Mais bordel!"*

GLAD TO BE rid of my cranky colleague, I lingered a moment on the balcony, considering how Antoine could be utterly blasé in the face of the most significant matters, and yet allow apparently trivial things to stir up the bile in him.

"What a conundrum," I thought. "And how will Antoine's disgrace ultimately come to an end at Bush House?"

Within the next hour, after the two-way, I finished packing my things. Without great effort, I had cleansed my mind of Antoine. And that interaction—although abrasive to my nerves—was easily forgotten. I needed to keep my priorities straight.

Later on, as I lay in bed waiting for sleep to come and steal me away into the folds of the night, I thought of the dangers that lay ahead, along the road to Baghdad. Realising that crossing my bridges before I got to them was unwise and distressful—a cumbersome obstacle to sleep—I turned to an infallible hack to empty my mind: prayer.

Chapter 15

CLEOPATRA'S NOSE

A motley cast. A full battalion of story hunters. Taken together, we certainly offered quite an impressive sight. More than twenty of us, BBC reporters and broadcast technicians, each with their bulky gears. We looked like we could overrun a poorly guarded city.

In the wider tale of the global coverage of the war, we played a part in a subplot of great significance— We drove home the point that the first-hand reporting of war was a privilege; one that was the exclusive province of big players in the media industry.

A cash-strapped news outlet would have crashed and burned, just by trying to put up a show like ours. Like sending David Attenborough to the Galápagos Islands for the *Life on Earth* series, there were things that only the BBC, funded by the *Licence Fee*, could afford; things that other news outlets, with their focus on profit margins, simply couldn't.

By God, if the British did anything that was yet to be properly imitated and equalled, it was the BBC. As one editor once proudly boasted to some young recruits, with a measure of truth, if the news were happening on the moon and there was just one media organisation that could get it, that probably would be the BBC.

The motley cast featured several household names of British journalism, who were not already embedded with the British or American troops. With us on this trip was Stephen Sackur, host of *HardTalk*, the BBC's flagship interviews programme. Also here was foreign correspondent Barbara Plett, whose regular bailiwick was the hotspots of Israel and the Palestinian Territories. Then there was Clare Marshall, a relatively fresh-faced up-and-comer who had joined the BBC as a freelancer three years earlier. She was out here, hoping to burnish her credentials with a view to advancing her personal ambition, which was to secure a much-coveted role as a regular news presenter on BBC television.

Yes, we were really a motley bunch. Count the drivers, and throw in the dozen of SAS officers, our security escorts, and our number could hit the 40 ballpark. And to fit us together—humans and gears and supplies of food, fuel, and water; to fit all of that in one single convoy, the SUVs had to number close to fourteen.

That was a lot of Pounds Sterling—certainly, enough to awaken the rage that was never extinct in the anti-Licence-Fee evangelists across Britain, those people who were certain that there was no point whatsoever to Auntie Beeb, a dinosaur. I have obvious reasons for not being a big fan of those anti-BBC evangelists. The Licence Fee is necessary to allow the BBC to produce unique and high-quality content. Without it, the BBC would be just another CNN.

As our impressive convoy set out and left Amman, rumbling away due east, I had plenty of time to spare. I throned totally idle in the rear seat of the four-wheeler, and with nothing to keep myself busy, I indulged in a silent wrestle with Blaise Pascal's cryptic statement about Cleopatra's nose. And as you will see, it wasn't random stuff.

THINKING OF PASCAL on one's way to the war. I know it's a bit of a curveball, but there's a point to this. First, some general context: I often resorted to *Pascal's Wager* to cut short any pesky arguments about the existence of God. Such arguments added nothing to the quality of my life, or to that of my family. They were a show of our hubris. They often ended up in more existential confusion, in more depression, and in ceaseless desperate quests for an alternative form of worship. The resulting idolatry could take many forms, such as drugs, sex, consumerism, identity tribalism, or simply the sound of one's own voice.

No, I am not a God fanatic. But of all the winding theories seeking to discount God, I have yet to see one that is a superior proposition. None of them are credible beyond the obvious stuff of the ego. Even some of the most respectable scientists I admire can turn into close-minded dogmatic prats when it comes to metaphysics. They always make the same inadequate argument: there is no evidence that God exists. Come on, *Faith is the substance of things hoped for, the evidence of things not seen.* And even though—to the believer—the evidence for God abounds, how the hell would it still be *faith* if the BBC could send out a TV crew to document it?

Ye of little faith, faith needs no evidence! And as Sherlock would tell Watson, *absence of evidence is not evidence of absence.*

No, I had long made a firm ruling on the matter of God's existence, so that I could free and allocate mental resources to other stuff.

And *Pascal's Wager* never failed to come in handy whenever some polemist came up to me, seeking to sell me their own existential confusion. Indeed, as the Frenchman argued, if you believe in God and—as a result—you lead a virtuous life, you will be rewarded with eternal happiness in heaven, if God does exist. Now, if ultimately God does not exist, how could leading a life of virtue be such a terrible loss?

Pascal's Wager was this plain, but sensible. Imagine how many wars Humanity would have made the economy of, if leaders and villains alike—*truly*, rather than hypocritically—conducted their lives on the assumption that there would ultimately be a divine reckoning? For example, if God were not just a political sale's pitch in Bush's mouth, how would he have reconciled any genuine reverence for the *Most High* with signing off this death-and-destruction campaign on the banks of the Tigris, especially on that rather fantastical concoction?

As I sat in the rear car seat in the convoy—musing on the *Wager*—it was clear to me that the philosopher's thought experiment on God was unimpeachable. And with idleness for company, I chose to further dwell on the man and his ideas. Next, I found myself puzzling over his little theory on Cleopatra's nose and Rome. And what's that?

Pascal argued that if Cleopatra's nose had been shorter, the course of history would have been different. It is a suggestion that the Queen's beauty—so compelling that she could dazzle Julius Caesar and Mark Anthony—had something to do with the rise of the Roman Empire. More than just superficial, the point of the Frenchman was that even a small event can have far-reaching implications.

And he was quite right: A difference of a few votes in Florida had put George W. Bush—rather than Al Gore—in the White House. Would there have been *Operation Iraqi Freedom* if Al Gore, the eco-activist, were the 43rd U.S. President?

Would there have been 9/11, if the new Republican Administration, taking over in January 2001, had not *demoted* Richard Alan Clarke—America's then-counter-terrorism tsar—whom the outgoing Clinton Administration had left a comprehensive anti-terror strategy?

As we can see, a tiny twist in the course of world events could indeed have tremendous implications.

In my rather *comparatively* trivial situation, as we proceeded on this long and tortuous journey towards Kuwait via the southern edge of Saudi Arabia, I stared at another example of how Pascal's argument checks out: Our seemingly accidental choice of a long and uncomfortable route to Baghdad.

If the Kingdom of Jordan, *this young country sitting on ancient land*, had not been half-hearted in its arrangements with the Coalition—collaborating with it in many other ways, but formally opposing the use of its territory for a land invasion of Iraq—our convoy, could have set a direct course from Amman, and striking straight for the city of Ramadi or Fallujah, we would have had a less punishing route to cover.

There is always a clear chain of causation.

Always.

And so much for Cleopatra's nose.

AS THOUGH A cosmic apprentice, with a mischievous streak, had been in charge of the clocks in the course of the night, our sleepover in Kuwait had been but a dash—gone, in the blink of an eye. I woke up groggy and still starved for sleep.

As I wondered where my Kuwaiti night might have gone, Amman and its magnificent rooftop panoramas seemed now so remote, as if they existed in another dimension, in an era long gone by. Time had seldom appeared this much of an illusion to me.

You've survived worst, I thought, as we gathered around the lead SAS officer for what would be a repeat of a now-familiar drill.

At bootcamp back in England, Captain Dorian Smith had drawn a parallel between this kind of safety brief and those pre-flight safeguarding instructions. He intended to underscore a common foolishness: Most air passengers rarely paid attention to the instructions performed for their benefit by dutiful air personnel. Air travel had got so safe that it has turned the common lot into a complacent bunch.

"But I tell you," Captain Dorian Smith had warned, *"A conflict zone is not the cabin of a Boeing 747. Unlike the air passenger, you must pay close attention to every damn safety brief."*

That scolding in the back of my mind did it for me. I suddenly felt more awake than I could have managed otherwise. I must stay alert. At a pinch, I could return to my sleep and play catch-up, when the convoy ultimately rolled out and hit the road again. No guarantee, there. The road ahead might be very rocky, in more than just a way.

The day before, having left the InterContinental at daybreak, our impressive convoy had kept striking eastward along macadam and dirt roads. Driving for fifteen long hours, we only took a few breaks either for wee or for stretch-ups. That was strongly advised by *Occupational Health*. And we had journeyed by the clear and cool air of the morning, and then into the dust-clouded heat of noon and beyond. It was already dusk when we arrived at last in Kuwait City. Not at the *Sheraton* that was booked full. But at a nearby hotel of a much lower standing—the Sheraton would have us on our way back home.

The three-star hotel was a haunt for journalists, foreign correspondents, international diplomats, military personnel, aid workers, and government officials. The City was close to Camp Doha, the main U.S. military base in Kuwait, which had been a staging post for the invasion of Iraq and was now the Coalition's main point of supply. This exposed the hotel to a lot of noise and light pollution. Kuwait is a small country, so the presence of the base and its personnel was overwhelming. The uninterrupted din of power generators was not audible from the hotel, but soldiers in uniform were everywhere. The hotel was frequently rattled by the disturbance of army aircraft taking off and landing. But this was not the only indication that these were exceptional times. Like the Sheraton, the complex was fortified for maximum security.

There were heavily guarded sentry posts, where anxious and humour-deprived privates, with buzz cuts, stood ready to open fire. There were concrete bulwarks that hinted at the possible fate of any suicide truck that foolishly attempted a brazen breach.

Sure, the venue had a *three stars* rating. But it was a jewel—one that was unfortunately marred by the atmosphere of war. Whatever tourist sites Kuwait City had to offer got little press here. Which was no trouble to us.

We had no time for tourism—or even for a good night's sleep. We only stopped over for the night because traveling under the cover of darkness would have increased our risk of dying a brutal death. Now, daybreak had come, and we were getting ready to hit the road again.

"It might not have seemed so to you," the SAS officer said as we stood by the idling SUVs in the large car park of the complex. "But the convoy covered dangerous ground yesterday."

Really? I wondered.

"We got here safe," the man continued, his accent more Essex than Leeds, more Russell Brand than Chris Moyles. "But yesterday, there was not a single moment along that route when we weren't a potential target for catastrophe."

At that, my heart skipped a beat, and I felt even more motivated to pay attention.

"Good planning, part of the reason for our extended

stopover in Amman, meant that officials in both Jordan and Saudi Arabia knew where we were likely to be at any time throughout the journey," he said. "That eliminated, I can now presume, any bad luck of being hit by some fighter jet. But compared to the road ahead, the journey from Amman was a picnic."

An aircraft overhead filled the morning's dry, cool air with a disheartening roar, suggesting how terrifying the last moments must have been for the unfortunate residents of Baghdad during those nights of "Shock and Awe", hearing an *F-15E Strike Eagle* so close before it unleashed its deadly payload below on their lodgings. It must have been far more earth-shattering than this mild roar. Yet, this mild roar was disruptive enough to our little assembly.

However loud our orator had proven himself to be, he was no match. Momentarily, he had to give way to the intrusive aircraft.

When the noise subsided, and just before the next thundering tumult tore through the morning, the man resumed his harangue.

From my time at bootcamp, I could anticipate most of his grim talking points. But he entertained us with such expert precision which I, of course, could not have commanded. He told us of the far too real risks of improvised explosive devices (IEDs), of unexploded rounds, of land mines, of ambushes at deceptive chokepoints, of sandstorms and of the desert's heat.

"Almost everything along our route ahead," he

said, pacing, and then marking a pause for effect, "—everything ahead potentially will conspire to kill you."

By now, I understood that the military might be the last bastion in the civilised world where sheer bluntness was delivered without batting an eyelid, without anyone at the receiving end collapsing into an emotional meltdown. It all made sense. What use would it be to spare your frail feelings, if you'd wind up dead? No, I no longer startled when I heard the *K-word,* and the *D-word.* To kill and to die—that was never remote in a soldier's universe. Sentiments were not ranked high here.

The officer continued relentlessly: "Everything, including our own side, is a mortal hazard. So, even with perfect discipline on your part, you will still need some damn good luck."

I should have bristled at his mention of *our own side.* Presumably, that was the side of the Coalition. But the truth was, we—the media—had no side in theory. We were neutral observers. But in reality, the circumstances had picked a side for us.

For God's sake, we were being escorted by SAS officers. And as we would find out later, Coalition soldiers shared their rations with us so we wouldn't starve. The inherent limits to our independence were becoming increasingly clear.

Rather than being intrigued that we had been assigned a side—whether by slip of tongue or by design—I felt a chill at the incisive truthfulness of the officer's argument: *Even with perfect discipline on your part, you still need some damn good luck.*

He couldn't have been more candid, as one recent incident served as a reminder of that sobering fact: In the early days of the military campaign, Terry Lloyd—a foreign correspondent for Britain's ITV channel—was traveling with a group of journalists near the city of Basra. At some point, their convoy came under fire. Terry was hit by a mortar shrapnel and later died of his injuries at a local hospital.

Tragic, obviously.

But it was all the more tragic for one reason. Just like the incident that would later send John Simpson's car up into the air, killing his translator; just like the shelling that would gut the balcony of the Palestine Hotel, killing Taras and José, the tragedy near Basra resulted from a friendly fire. Terry's convoy took that deadly round from U.S. troops.

"There's little you can do about a friendly air missile tumbling down your way," our SAS minder now told our assembly. "But you can avoid being shot, when at one of the many checkpoints we will be coming across. And here's how: Don't act smart; let sniffer dogs be your friends; don't argue with military personnel who ask you questions. Remember, these checkpoints are designed to prevent the movement of enemy combatants, to intercept any flow of weapons and supplies. You are not the enemy. Don't act like you are."

The advancing sun had rolled up the remaining

curtain of night, and morning light had crept upon us while we were absorbed in the briefing. By the time the orator clapped his hands to signal our departure, the sun was pressing down its early rays through the cool, still morning air.

When the sun climbed high enough above the city horizon, our convoy pulled out and soon attacked the *Tarīq Al-Mawt*—that highway of gruesome reputation.

Chapter 16

THE HIGHWAY OF DEATH

No fewer than three hours had elapsed since our convoy left behind *The Highway of Death*, striking ahead. Now, the cavalcade, rather gently and *very* carefully, came to a halt. We were coming down for yet another *checkpoint treatment*. It was a nerve-racking experience. If only because of what met the wayfarer's eye at first sight—an ugliness of some unique kind.

Before you follow us through this razor wire and concertina barrier, let's address what would be an obvious gap if left unaddressed—*The Highway of Death*.

TARĪQ AL-MAWT. IT is the Arabic denomination of an exceedingly infamous highway, a six-lane stretch of road leading north out of Kuwait. It is a legacy of the first Gulf War—a brutal token, by which Saddam Hussein was to remember that invading a neighbouring country, one under the protective wings of the United States, was a naughty bid that must never *again* be attempted.

The Highway of Death.

When Saddam Hussein laid heavy into Kuwait that fateful year of 1990, the United States built a case for intervention. Washington successfully sold it to 35 other countries. Soon, a coalition was born. Under *Operation Desert Storm,* the ensuing response to Saddam's transgression went on to be a spectacular display of deadly fireworks. *Desert Storm* was a punishment of high proportion. It subjected the invading forces, first, to intense airstrikes. Then, to a blistering ground assault.

Ultimately, the firepower of the coalition forced the invaders to retreat. It had sent them hot into a hasty escape across the desert, through clouds of billowing dust. That desperate dash for safety would remain just that. The Iraqis' hope of using the six-lane roadway to haul out equipment, and supplies, and troops was a dead end—*literally*. Quite simply, the US-led coalition wouldn't allow it. The Coalition would turn the anticipated escape route into a graveyard. Fates were sealed when American aircrafts kicked high into the sky, showering missiles and bombs down on the retreating convoys.

Ghastly.

After the airstrikes, the road was strewn with bodies and body parts, and the desert landscape was disfigured by the charred remains of vehicles and equipment. It all testified to the intensity of the attacks. But how many people died in that inferno?

There has never been any agreement on the exact number of casualties. Estimates put it somewhere between many hundreds to several thousand. There is no disagreement, however, as to the fact that civilians were caught up in the terrible slaughter. The *Geneva Conventions*—some convincingly argue—might have been violated.

In any event, *The Highway of Death*—a grisly symbol of the human cost of war—never ceased to fuel debates about the ethics of warfare.

I had seen the grim footage of the devastation several times before, but nothing gives as much realism to this haunting *lore* as travelling in person along the route. All these years later—despite the attempts at cleaning up the rusty mess—burned-out tanks, and trucks, and other vehicles still littered the highway. To travel here in person opens you up to a *heart-level* understanding of why *The Highway of Death* is a cautionary tale, reminding us that international disagreements are better resolved through diplomacy and other peaceful means.

But then again, this was 2003. And this, *again*, was war. Again, a US-led coalition was back fighting Iraqi forces.

As our convoy made its way along this corridor of gruesome reputation, I remember thinking that the enduring reminder of the *Tarīq Al-Mawt* was a total waste. More troubling to me than the actual disregard for the lessons of recent past was that—this time around—the warriors-in-chief, George Bush, and Tony Blair, had deliberately brought death and destruction to the Iraqis on a carefully constructed *pack of lies*.

We are bound to repeat history when we don't give a hoot about it.

THE IMPENDING CHECKPOINT inspection was nerve-wracking. Everything about it was ugly and aggressive. At first, that was a feeling. Then, it was down to that barrier. A sight of an unpoetic alliance of concrete, razor wire, and sandbags. It was also the fleet of Humvees and the nervous soldiers manning machine guns and other deadly weapons. *Experience* at the checkpoint was that of volatility—a rugged affair.

Reminiscent of the shifting frontier in Far West folktales, the checkpoint was a place that was tight with the tension of distrust; a place where people felt uneasy and suspicious around each other. At the checkpoint, *humanity* seemed to be on a perpetual trial, teetering on the brink of collapse. One small incident at the checkpoint, like a spark in a hydrogen combustion chamber, could quickly lead to a deadly gunfight.

In a war zone, it is natural for soldiers to be paranoid and to shoot first and ask questions later. But in Iraq, the paranoia firmly took hold in early April, when some Iraqis were still celebrating the toppling of Saddam Hussein's statue. This change in attitude was triggered by a suicide truck bombing in a Shia suburb of Baghdad. And now, we were dealing with the seemingly endless consequences of that bombing. And here we were, ready to undergo yet another thorough and tense inspection.

I had not yet properly surveyed the cityscape, but I knew that we had just arrived in Najaf, the Shia Holy City. We had covered more distance than was left to cover. A little under a hundred miles to the north lay Baghdad, a chaotic mess that we had yet to discover. But my mind was not yet on the big, bruised city.

I was stuck in a sort of loop, brooding over *The Highway of Death*. Its disturbing awe had been with me even as we coasted into Safwan, the border city captured early by the Coalition and used as a major staging outpost for the initial stage of *Operation Iraqi Freedom;* its disturbing awe had been with me even as we arrived in Nasiriyah, site of one of the fiercest battles of the war. But I must say that in Nasiriyah, the sight of the rubble and deserted streets was so fresh and aggressive that it grabbed my attention and forced me out of my brooding. I found myself surveying the damage the city had endured. I knew that it would make good fodder for a speedy file to London. I needed to gather as much detail as I could, without disrupting the schedule or route of our unwieldy convoy.

Nasiriyah was a strategic military objective, with its many bridges over the Euphrates River providing open passages to various parts of the country. The Coalition had to capture it at all costs, in order to deliver a major psychological blow to Saddam's forces and keep the operation's timeline on track. The foreign troops achieved their goal after several days of fighting, but not without a cost. Up to 40 of them laid down their lives in action.

The events of Nasiriyah would undoubtedly alter the collective narrative of the locals. There was something about it that would stay with them for a long time to come. The stigmas were on full display for wayfarers like us to see, to feel, and to reflect upon as we took our notes.

And as I surveyed the many damaged or destroyed buildings, I wondered—sticking to the terms of our mission—about the fate of the innocent civilians who could have been trapped inside.

Were they killed? If not, where could they be now?

Wherever they were, they must have experienced unimaginable trauma, from which they may never fully recover.

Nasiriyah, this battered city, had kept me in the *now*, with the sheer depth of its wounds. But as the convoy started moving again, a reflective monotony returned, along with the same haunting introspections, fuelled by the pervasive atmosphere of death and dying.

I was deep in such a long spell of restive introspection

when we rolled into Najaf. I could have stayed lost in thought if it weren't for the G.I. in battle fatigues who, with his combat rifle drawn and at the ready, made his way up the queue of SUVs and stopped next to ours, giving the boot a single, definitive *bang*.

Our Egyptian driver, *Imad Fadheel*, was young and fit. He knew the drill and quickly got out of the car and popped the boot open, as requested.

The G.I. held out his hand in a firm gesture, indicating that the boot should be left open. Imad theatrically complied. Then, the armed American soldier moved up the queue, bearing down on his next target.

After having already worked our way through those major checkpoints in Nasiriyah and Samawah, we were now familiar with this whole choreography, although the Americans kept their checkpoint rules of engagement shrouded in secrecy. In standard cases not involving rogue travellers that ignored commands and bore straight into the barrier, we knew that the enforcement of security at the checkpoint unfolded in a chain.

This G.I. was just a forerunner. If he had spotted a suicide bomber or a booby trap, he would have raised an alarm, even though it could have meant his own death. His bravery would have spared the lives of his fellow soldiers. Now, since he had found no danger, the rest of the inspection chain unfolded. And even with our SAS minders around, we weren't given an easy pass at any of the checkpoints. The security barrier always remained in place until we had satisfied them that we were who we claimed to be—journalists on legitimate business.

It was a little past 3:00 p.m. in Najaf when the SUV in front of us was cleared to pass through the checkpoint. A soldier of some rank, well at ease but very business-like, approached our vehicle. His swift eyes darted around as he focused on his German shepherd he had on a leash. The man was covered on both flanks by two rifle-toting servicemen. Overall, nerves were kept in check, likely due to the fact that we all spoke English. Iraqis who spoke little or no English at all risked being treated roughly or even shot at Coalition checkpoints.

Imad the driver, on the advice of our SAS minders, had climbed back into the driver's seat. The American shepherd's master bent down to level his eyes with Imad and greeted him sharply, "Good afternoon. Could you, please, roll down all the windows?"

Imad—as theatrically as only *he* knew how—beamed at him. The English of the Egyptian was perfect. But he only used it when strictly necessary, when it was more productive to speak rather than just act. He heard the "please", but he knew not to be fooled by it. This was more of an instruction than a plea. Silently, he complied. And the windows went down on all sides.

The American peered into the driver's side of the car. Then, seemingly satisfied that it was safe for the dog to enter, he turned to us and said, "Can you all grab your IDs and step out onto the sidewalk?"

A moment later, we were all out of the car, standing a step or two away. We watched as the dog, excited and eager, hoisted itself up on its hind legs and lurched into the SUV. Its humid muzzle, dutifully downcast, darted about, probing above and below the car's seats. The dog's master monitored its exertion with intense alertness.

Me, too. And as I watched, the urgency in the dog's fevered demeanour had me worried that it might actually sniff out something illegitimate, even though I was certain that was impossible. I was relieved when the dog stepped back out of the car, whining almost imperceptibly as though disappointed for turning up nothing.

Before clearing us through the barrier and moving on to the next vehicle, the inspector, still flanked by his rifle-toting colleagues, took care of one last formality. He diligently scanned our passports one at a time, shifting his severe gaze up and down to compare our real-life faces to the photos in the documents. The repetitive routine seemed as redundant as the overriding question that played as a choppy soundtrack to it: "What's your business here?"

Our mission in Iraq? A redundant question.

He had already established that we were from the BBC, here to report on the war. I guess that asking redundant questions was part of the protocol, which he was too orthodox to break. So, he stuck to his routine of scanning IDs and asking redundant questions.

When he drew up by my side, he took my passport, opened it, and started to read it.

"Venuste—"

He stopped, stumped over my surname.

"Nshimiyimana," I slowly articulated, with a humourless smile. Who knew if they might suddenly take an actual smile for an evil trick, which could be deadly. I couldn't be too much on my bloody guards. "Venuste Alexandre Nshimiyimana," I added for whatever it was worth.

The inspector shone one *special-issue* glance at me and scoffed. "A hell of a name, if you ask me."

"I get that a lot," I said, again faking humour, chuckling awkwardly. "There's an entire club of good folks who can't say my name. So, you are actually very much welcome."

Quickly perusing my passport, the man almost immediately returned it to me. "Where in Africa, buddy?" he asked, cocking his rigid brow at me.

Okay. Considering that my passport was *Belgian*—and there was no doubt about it—I took the liberty to assume that the American shepherd's master was talking *origins*. That was fine. *So let's do origins, then.*

"Rwanda," I told him. "The Country of a Thousand Hills."

"Whoa," he said, his eyelids flying up, treating me to another intently glance. Perhaps, it was a sign that he was impressed by the picture he might have conjured up of some *African country with a thousand hills*. Anyway, he didn't break his step as he moved away from me. And before he held out his hand for the next passport due for his scrutiny, he added as though regretfully: "Rwanda? Never been. Maybe, someday. Thanks for being sport!"

WHEN WE FINALLY left Najaf and headed further north, I found myself thinking of that unexpectedly kind inspector, a proverbial swallow. I wondered what it would be like to meet that G.I. again someday in Rwanda, but I quickly dismissed the idea. The chances of me ever running into him in Kigali were worse than slim. Anyway, before that whole anecdotal encounter eventually sank into some obscure recess of my mind, I made a point of scolding myself. I didn't want it to re-emerge as an embarrassing slip of a tongue in my reporting.

"*Look here, Venuste,*" I thought. "*At checkpoints across Iraq, the standard treatment is that you'd likely be hailed with bullets for a misplaced wink. Don't mistake some random personal pleasant experience for the lot of the poor Iraqi people.*"

As our convoy cruised on the last segment of our journey, with Baghdad now closer than ever, I remembered that there was probably worse going on in this country than the ruggedness of life at the checkpoint.

PART III

I noticed one of the tanks had its barrel pointed up at the building. We went inside and there was an almighty crash. That tank shell, if it was an American tank shell, was aimed directly at this hotel and directly at journalists. This wasn't an accident. It seems to be a very accurate shot.

—DAVID CHATER
Foreign Correspondent, Baghdad

Chapter 17

THE COMPLEX IN RASHEED DISTRICT

Its location close to the *Tigris River* offered a scenic view of the waterway. That must have been a great unique selling point in those olden days of peace. Now, it sat in volatile territory. Sounds of gunfire and explosions echoed in from corners that were not all remote, blinding and numbing the senses, casting a hue of brutality over any beauty that could have been there to behold; over any splendour that could have whisked the beholder into a vortex of escapism.

For over a month, this complex in the Harun Al-Rasheed district of Baghdad had haunted my nights, especially on the eve of my outbound flight from London. All those hypothetical thoughts about the worst that could happen to me had mentally fast-tracked me here. I was never bold enough to confess it to myself, but I had feared all along that I would never see this place. The journey was long. And the road dangerous.

Fortunately, we'd now survived both the journey and the road. And here it was—*The Palestine Hotel*.

How the hell did we finally make it here? And why would we be checking out only a day later? Okay, let's not jump the gun.

As you will see, any account of the Iraq War—a war that was as much about military tactics as it was about the control of public perception—would be woefully incomplete without the story of *The Palestine Hotel*.

Chapter 18

BAGHDAD IS FALLING

The sun in the brooding sky of Baghdad was now close to the zenith, about to flatten the tormented shadows across the city. The yellow glare of daylight flared and darted down with relentless intensity into the murky waters of the Tigris River. The *Shock-And-Awe* aerial campaign had now come to an end. The initial phase of *Operation Iraqi Freedom* had been brief. Now, the down-and-dirty ground battle that was under way had entered a crucial stage.

A few days earlier, the *Third Infantry Division* of the US Army had run the gauntlet of Iraqi artillery fire to capture the city's airport. Along the way, Coalition forces had encountered the stiffest resistance of the invasion so far. But the battle for the airport seemed to have marked the end of the Iraqi Forces as a functionally coordinated and coherent entity. The operational divisions of the *Republican Guards* were now in disarray; the *Fedayeen As-Saddam*, the militia of self-sacrificers who stood ready to lay down their lives for the Iraqi dictator and his family, were stunned into dysfunctional bewilderment; and most of the country's heavy artillery and Saddam's fleet of T-72 and T-62 tanks had been put out of use.

The tide had truly begun to turn with the Battle of the Karbala Gap, a fiercely fought episode of the war that allowed US troops to breach the last line of defence between Baghdad and the advancing Coalition forces. With the clearing of the Karbala Gap, the Americans seized and secured the Al-Kaeda Bridge, using it to operate a hasty crossing over the Euphrates River, the last natural obstacle before the city.

Sure, the Americans lost a few men in the Battle of the Karbala Gap, but the biggest casualty was the *Madina Division* of the Iraqi Army. The Coalition had failed to destroy this unit in an earlier attempt, which resulted in the shooting-down of a US attack helicopter and the capture of its two-man crew, who were later paraded on television.

Touted as the topmost unit of the *Republican Guards*, with the best training and the most potent military hardware available to Saddam, the *Medina Division* was tasked with the impossible mission of guarding the Karbala Gap against American penetration. The local Fedayeen and fighters from the *Nebuchadnezzar*

Division were on hand to provide reinforcement, but the elite warriors failed in their mission to stem the progress of the US troops. Their division technically ceased to exist as a fully coordinated unit.

With aerial cover from the US *Delta Force* and the British SAS, the American *Third Infantry Division*, having learned from their previous debacle, struck at the *Republican Guards* with everything they had. By the time they secured the bridge, over 700 Iraqi soldiers had been killed and more than 30 *T-72* tanks had been bombed into useless scrap metal.

The Battle of the Karbala Gap had thrown wide open the road to Baghdad. With the breach of this last rampart, a lengthy column of American M1A1 Abrams tanks, Bradley attack vehicles, and M113 armoured personnel carriers drilled forward, bound for the airport where the *de-Saddamisation* of Baghdad would soon begin.

Vincent Brooks, spokesman of the US Central Command, announced the capture of the airport shortly after it happened. He told reporters, "The airport formerly known as *Saddam International Airport* has a new name—*Baghdad International Airport*. And it is a gateway to the future of Iraq." Vincent Brooks's enthusiasm would have been more guarded if he could have anticipated the explosion of tribal violence that would flare up in the months ahead.

As the Americans set out to turn the freshly renamed airport into a tactical command center for the looming

Battle of Baghdad, they couldn't believe how easily things had gone up to that point. Most intriguing, they had seen nothing yet of the Weapons of Mass Destruction that they had dreaded most. And the easy meltdown of the Iraqi defence lines around Baghdad seemed too good to be true. They wondered: Could Baghdad be *a trap, a clever ruse, or just a hollow shell?*

Well, the Americans needed to make sure. They needed to test what remained of Saddam's defences.

The day following the capture of the airport, commanding officers ordered an armoured raid deep into Baghdad. The task force departed from a previously secured location south of the city and pushed down Highway 8 towards the airport, where they linked up with the *First Brigade* of the US *Third Infantry Division*, the combat unit that had taken control of the airport a day earlier and turned it into a tactical command centre. Operation *Thunder Run One* was thus complete, a risky operation that encountered little resistance.

Iraqi fighters confronted the task force with light weaponry, hitting only the rear of a tank with an RPG shell and setting it ablaze. Unfazed, the task force pressed ahead, calling a friendly strike against the tank to prevent it from becoming a trophy for the Iraqi Army, as that Apache helicopter shot down three weeks earlier in Karbala had become. Despite this, Iraqi Minister of Information Muhammad Saeed al-Sahhaf conveniently went on television to claim the destruction of the tank as an act of valour on the part of Iraqi troops and evidence that America was having trouble in Baghdad.

The real trouble would come several months later.

But at this point, Saeed al-Sahhaf—whom the Americans had nicknamed the *Bob of Baghdad* because he could tell a blatant lie with a straight face—was simply doing his job: spreading propaganda. And that was fair game under the circumstances. After all, Coalition forces had only moved this fast, well ahead of schedule, thanks to an elaborate use of feint tactics that had left the Republican Guards constantly wavering and indecisive about where the US troops would strike next.

Operation *Thunder Run One* turned out to be a drill, testing and paving the way for a similar Operation—*Thunder Run Two*.

Thunder Run Two, which had begun a day earlier, reached a turning point on Tuesday, 8th April 2003, as the *Second Brigade* of the US *Third Infantry Division* bullied its way into the heart of the Iraqi capital. The capture of the government districts, the prize at sight, was now within reach, but it was not yet a done deal.

Even in disarray, the *Republican Guards* and the *Fedayeen* were taking a brave last stand. Bloodied but unbowed, they were still in combat, taking cover and playing a mortal game of hide-and-seek with the American troops.

But where was Saddam Hussein?

If the dictator were still in Baghdad, neither Bush nor his Secretary of Defence, Donald Rumsfeld, wanted him out of town anymore. Like the airport and the government districts, America now wanted to capture him. They had prepared a long rap sheet of offences dating back to the 1980s. He now had to answer for his transgressions. He must not run. But the dictator was already on the run.

Having taken to his heels and fled towards his hometown of Tikrit—as it later transpired—he had long crossed the Victory Archway of *Quaws An-Nasr* beyond which stood the Palace. All of it would soon disappear within the ring of blast-proof concrete walls of the future Green Zone. By now, Saddam in his full flight, must have understood that Baghdad was ripe for a fall. And Baghdad would fall a day later—Baghdad fell on 9th April.

As the city gasped for breath in the heat of the overwhelming uncertainty; while any radial sweep around the city no longer showed the towering columns of dark billowing clouds of acrid smoke from the "Shock and Awe" campaign; while from above and below, the city seemed to hold nothing but terror for the wise and the foolish, the Tigris lay seemingly unafraid in its bed.

Impervious to the groaning rumble of change, the river casually snaked through the city, keeping it split into two, just as it did dutifully when the Abbasid Caliphs still ruled over Baghdad more than a thousand years ago. The Tigris was somewhat of a cold, unwilling, silent witness.

Forlorn and barren, and relieved of the usual hustle and bustle in this city of five million souls, countless bridges straddled the placid river, throwing themselves across from bank to bank, rather wearing an air of intensity that spoke of a premature End of Times.

One of those bridges was the *Al Jumhuria*—the tragic *Al Jumhuria* Bridge.

But at this point, the bridge had no inkling that it was about to become the stage for a most reported tragedy.

Chapter 19

THE KILLER ROUND

In better days, the visitor from the eastern side of the Tigris, heading to the executive heart of the city, would have found a most direct route across the *Al Jumhuria* Bridge, which firmly held its ground over the river under the beating sun. Obviously, this Tuesday was none of those better days. But this Tuesday was one decisive day.

At this stage of the Battle of Baghdad, the Coalition troops were yet to consolidate their control of the city. They were up against an enemy that feared no loss any longer. Those still lurking in the gutted buildings across this part of the city—the die-hard Saddam loyalists—were not fighting to live. No, they believed in death. They saw valour in being killed while making Baghdad a maximum hell for the American invaders.

Before the sun climbed up this high, some 500 of these fierce fighters had ventured out of their makeshift haunts and bunkers. Spotting the U.S. *Third Infantry Division* marking its territory on the edges of the government districts, they went at them from across the bridge, from all sides of the bridge. Quickly, the intensity of RPG and mortar shelling, the blast of rounds from AK-47s, would force the U.S. troops into a retreat—a tactical retreat just for the time to call in some air strikes.

Soon, *A-10 Warthog* fighter jets were in the sky. They unleashed fire, discharged devastating payloads, with bombs falling from the sky at intervals of five to eight seconds. It wasn't long before a fresh column of dark plume arose into the brooding, vaulted sky of Baghdad, marking the spot to be seen from afar.

Elsewhere, across the Tigris, Al-Jazeera correspondent—Tarek Ayoub—and his cameraman had stood on the roof of the network's bureau reporting on the spike in the combats. At some point, a fighter jet, which was part of the air fleet in action, engaged in a series of evasive manoeuvres: It dipped in and out of the low cover of cloud that hung over the bridge; it dropped high-temperature flares to bait away smart missiles; it performed acrobatic twists and turns to make itself a hard target. Then, it levelled up above the Al-Jazeera building. Next, it dropped an air-to-surface missile below, hitting the structure.

Perhaps, Tarek Ayoub never heard the roar of the

Warthog when it lined above him. The reporter—who had only been in town for three days, having travelled from his permanent base in the Jordanian capital Amman—was knocked unconscious when the missile made impact. He was perhaps already dead when they lowered his blanket-draped body in the back of a reporter's van, which started off for one of the local hospitals that overflowed with the influx of war casualties.

Back on the bridge, when the *Warthogs* ultimately went quiet, lifeless bodies of about 50 Iraqi fighters were found littering the smoke-filled combat theatre. The survivors had melted away under the raids. But the U.S. troops knew this was not over.

Now, if the enemy combatants were to mount a fresh showdown later, the Americans wanted to make sure it didn't happen here again. The *Al Jumhuria* Bridge must be fastened into a secure lockdown. For one thing, the bridge and its surroundings sat on the borders of the future seat of the *Coalition Provisional Authority*.

A quick lockdown was necessary.

Shortly after the brazen counter-attack, three American *M1A1 Abrams* tanks made a compelling production of themselves, rolling majestically into position at the western end of the bridge. From their vintage point, any hostile movement further afield would squarely fall within their lethal field of fire. Any advancing assailant, mounted or on foot, would be knocked into a ball of flames with a timely, carefully targeted discharge of a tank round.

FROM ACROSS THE river on the eastern bank of the Tigris at the balconies of that 17-storey building, the American tanks stationed at the *Al Jumhuria* Bridge were being surveyed. In that high-rise—*the Palestine Hotel*—a fraternity of reporters were at work. These were not the *embeds* who reported from within the ranks of troops in live combat zones. These men and women were part of teams deployed here from around the world. If you saw *non-army* footage on television about the Battle of Baghdad, it was likely that some media operative here had caught it on camera, putting their lives on the line.

Now—alerted by the latest skirmishes from the opposite bank of the river—the journalists trained their sights on the American tanks. They wondered about that fresh rising plume of smoke. *What was the target? Was there any casualty?*

Military spokespersons would soon provide the details. At least, what they would choose to communicate. But beforehand, the reporters could read the familiar tell-tale signs of death. And this far from the bridge, they felt relatively safe. Well, as safe as anyone in Baghdad right now could reasonably hope to be.

After all, they were the nosy busybodies in this war—they were as indiscreet as they were meddlesome.

Every side in the conflict did its best to keep them in check: Coalition forces were irritated that they often gave too many details, threatening to foil some of their battle plans. They wished they reported as little as possible about their blunders, of which there were *and again would be* many.

To the Iraqi forces, the guests at the Palestine Hotel stood, by default, on the wrong side of the war—the invaders' side. "Just look carefully," Saddam's Information Minister, Saeed al-Sahhaf, once remonstrated at them. "I only want you to look carefully. Do not repeat the lies of liars. Do not become like them."

At the BBC, we certainly had a good idea of Saddam's opinion of Western media outlets. In the lead-up to the invasion, quite displeased with the work of Caroline Hawley—at the time, the BBC Correspondent in Baghdad—Saddam's men took the decision to revoke her credentials and run her out of the country. Caroline would have the last laugh in some way, since she would return into the country in time for the fall of Tikrit, Saddam's hometown.

Before Caroline's ultimate triumph over censorship, the BBC had to replace her with a young man named Rageh Omar. Then, the pressure shifted camps.

Omar—an Oxford-educated Brit; a Muslim of Somali origin—was conservative when it came to the BBC's sacrosanct tradition of impartiality. He would reflect the views of the Iraqi side of the conflict, just as he reported on the talking points of the US

Central Command. He would go on to become the most prominent face in the Western coverage of the Invasion, notable for his display of compassion and balance. Rageh Omar was careful to eschew the dramatic style of American reporters embedded with the US troops, who tended to portray the war as a Hollywood movie featuring bad guys and good guys.

For his staunch attachment to impartiality, the young reporter would ironically become the target of a whispering campaign among British government officials, who questioned his loyalties. It was a shameful slander, and it foreshadowed the looming clash between the BBC and Tony Blair's Downing Street in the tragic David Kelly Affair that was yet to break.

This is my point: the obstacles in the way of these correspondents at *The Palestine Hotel* were not just the tanks and the war planes with their rounds and missiles. The obstacles were also psychological, political. A reporter intent on properly doing his job in an unyielding manner was an enemy of either party in the conflict or both. The sad old dictum about war and the truth remained unimpeachable. If the truth is not obscured through spin-doctoring or blatant lies and manipulation, it will be by other means— the threat of death or being injured, either physically or psychologically. In other words, to be wielding a microphone, a recorder, a camera anywhere in this suffocating God-forsaken city was a foolish dance of a kind with fate. And as the tragic death of Tarek

Ayoub demonstrates, there were many brutal ways this flirtation with danger could end.

As the journalists studied the thick, acrid smoke that billowed into the sky, with the M1 tanks clearly within their sight, they were oblivious to the fact that they had triggered an alarm. They knew not that a US tank commander had caught a suspicious sight posted at a balcony of the hotel; a sighting that had sent the armoured platoon into a frenzy. Unbeknownst to the *fraternity*, the tank commanders were frantically communicating with each other. Decisions were being made.

And when the ensuing tragedy hit, the weapon for the *double homicide* was an American *M1A1 Abrams* tank.

THROUGH THE BROODING sky of Baghdad, midday was looming large and hot when the U.S. tank battalion on the bridge started to spy on communications in Arabic between Iraqi forces. The Americans had previously taken hold of a radio from a fallen team of Saddam's *Republican Guards*. The little toy was now proving very useful.

As the Americans listened on, they quickly realised that something nasty was being cooked up. From the gist of an embedded intel officer who provided instant translation, they established that an Iraqi *spotter* was directing enemy combatants for a fresh onslaught on the U.S. troops. Any subsisting doubt fell away when the battalion suddenly came under RPG shelling and mortar fire. Taking out the invisible *spotter* literally became a matter of life and death.

In the frantic effort to locate and neutralise the enemy *asset*, tank commanders raised binoculars, scanning around. Across the river, a silhouette at a balcony on the fifteenth floor of the Palestine Hotel came within the line of sight of tank commander Philip Wolford. A brief urgent exchange ensued. And Capt. Wolford felt sure they had *spotted* the bloody Iraqi forward observer. Whether the captain sought counsel from his top boss, General David Perkins—a Brigade Commander within the U.S. *Third Infantry Division*—that was lost to history. But action was not delayed.

As the clock was about to strike noon, the press corps at the *Palestine Hotel* looked on in absolute horror, as Capt. Wolford swung around the turret of his tank, then took aim and fired a high-explosive round into their shelter. The shell flew in and crashed into that fifteenth-floor balcony. The question immediately was not whether the incident was fatal—It was rather how many were killed and who.

When the cloud of smoke and dust began to settle, the answer was clear: The casualties were Taras Protsyuk, a Reuters cameraman, and José Couso a Spanish television freelancer. The shell had left them with fatal injuries. Medics were called. But the trip to the hospital was rather for the mortuary. Taras and José could not be saved.

With this double tragedy, the Battle of Baghdad—just

in one single day—thus claimed altogether the lives of three members of the press corps. Tuesday, 8th April 2003 suddenly stood apart as the deadliest day for reporters since the war began. It was a sad day for journalism.

RIGHT FROM THE start, Iraq was never to be a media black hole, but it was clear that each party to the conflict would be fighting the parallel battle for the control of the narrative.

Along the way, the media would become a target—one way or another. And here we were: The price for keeping the brutal realities of this war before the eyes of the world was already costly. And this Tuesday, it just ran even higher.

Chapter 20

AHLAN WA SAHLAN

Long weeks of fearful anticipation had elapsed since the tragedy at *The Palestine Hotel* and here, I was at last. Our convoy had just crossed the entrance into Baghdad. Shortly, I would join the ranks of the guests at the *wounded* complex. That was if our convoy cleared the last hurdles on the way.

THE SETTING SUN had made a bloody mess of the city landscape and was about to retract its fiery blanket for the sake of the falling evening. Having entered the breathless metropolis from the *Abu Ghraib Gate* in the western outskirts, our cavalcade was spared the need to deploy visors. The flare of the retreating sun conveniently shone at the convoy from behind, casting oblique shadows that run ahead of us.

We didn't need to strain our eyes to take in the quite prominent scars the Iraqi Capital had sustained.

With the glimmering rays of the setting sun clear of our line of sight, we could tell with no shade of a doubt that Baghdad was a *great casualty of war*. Along our path, the evidence for the recent violence was overwhelming. Here and there, we could see charred remains of heavy artillery pieces, carbon-black carcasses of cars and pickup trucks, piles of rubble, disfigured buildings—some now just a little more than standing brick and mortar sieves. Amid the mess, forlorn palm trees that had survived the fighting swayed in the desolate air of the late afternoon.

However, Baghdad was not as much a shattered giant China Shop through which an elephant might have stomped.

No, less than that, the city offered the sight of a beast knocked breathless off its feet. In other words, there was no suggestion of the nasty indiscriminate punishment exacted years earlier, and to which *The Highway of Death* was a sobering testimony. The roadsides had their share of bodies in advanced decomposition, but they had not been turned into graveyards. Of course, the evidence of the Coalition's *blunt-force* take-over of the city was on display. And beyond the shroud of simmering tension, Baghdad lay vulnerable to the ripple of the coming *aftershock* that would later rumble on for years.

Risking blunder from the Coalition or ambush

on the part of the last men standing from Saddam's army, our convoy slowly drilled through, descending from the suburbs down towards the heart of the city—towards the *Harun Al-Rasheed* district.

Shortly before we drove across the city gate, I was struck by a glaring irony. Spelled out in Arabic and English, a road sign did its best in extending a promise of hospitality to us. WELCOME TO BAGHDAD, the sign proclaimed.

Sadly, the congenial message failed to elicit in me the predictable excitement I normally experienced upon crossing the boundaries of any new city. Rather than excitement, it set my pulse running a little faster.

Welcome? I thought. *But welcome to what? To our possible death?*

To be honest, I wasn't sure what I wanted the road sign to say. Perhaps, I was surprised instinctually that it was there at all; that it was not torn down by some *Fedayeen* fighter, hopelessly intent on not marking up the limits of Baghdad for easy identification by the invading armies.

When we pulled up at last in front of *The Palestine Hotel*, I was taken aback to be welcomed by the same effusive message of hospitality, this time on the part of *actual* residents of the city, who had to lie low as the *Warthog* fighter jets flew around dropping bombs.

"*Ahlan wa sahlan,*" they chanted.

That's Arabic for *Welcome.*

Again, I wondered, "*Welcome to what?*"

I would soon discover there was method to this madness. The arrival into Baghdad of *free-willing* outsiders, with no business to do with the invading armies, was taken for something of a solidarity. Moreover, we represented a promise of employment for people who so badly wanted to work.

As it happened, we had unwittingly brought false hope into this place where *Doomsday* seemed to have arrived much ahead of those scriptural End Times.

I DID NOT immediately look for evidence of the damage sustained by the complex, because something more urgent claimed my attention straight away. The front yard of *The Palestine Hotel* was mayhem. It was packed with *far too many* idle residents who had very little to do with their time.

Hawkers had camped here and were staying put for the foreseeable future. They had extended the front of the hotel into a mini-market of sorts. And from their makeshift positions, they flogged anything that could be of vital use in this city of shortages. From alcohol to foods; watches to paintings; *Nokia* phone covers to flash lamps—they sold anything that could fetch a British Pound or an American Dollar. And the clientele was of course the crowd of foreign correspondents and aid workers. And what was advertised to reporters here was not just those piles of *bric-a-brac*. Some who were confident in their bilingual skills lingered in this *marketplace* with hope, literally praying to *Allah* for an opportunity to tout their wares—or services, rather—ready to serve as interpreters, as fixers.

The hawkers and service providers, once and again, kicked into a flurry of excitement at every new arrival of a vehicle. As it were, we almost aroused a riot when our convoy glided along and came to a stop in front of the complex. Had it not been for the hotel's heavy security detail, we would have been overrun by this rag-tag of traders who offered too many things we had no immediate need of.

It broke my heart to see this much competition for the *welcoming* of us, which was viewed as a massive *vacancy opening*. Like in any situation where the *supply* outstripped the *demand*, the mini-market in front of *The Palestine Hotel* was a damn place of fierce competition.

And while the situation warranted my heartbreak, I was committing a fundamental breach of safety protocol by surrendering to sentimentalism. My wallowing in pity for this innocent crowd was a distraction; it lowered my guard.

As per our hostile environment training at bootcamp, I was supposed never to forget that stationary crowds like this one amounted to a big-time security hazard. How?

Who could say, for sure, that everybody in this makeshift mini-market was a hawker with a legitimate hope of securing some odd job? No, this was the sad truth: The most pitiful of the faces who stared at us with empty eyes could turn out to be a mean suicide bomber. And that, I would soon remember and adjust my conduct accordingly.

But before I did, I succumbed to the innocence of a boy who had fixed an eloquent gaze at me, looking out from the crowd that was kept at bay by the hotel's security—Security just wouldn't risk our safety by granting unvetted *porters* their wish to carry our loads into the hotel's lobby. There was more trusted help at hand for that.

"Hi," I said, waving remotely at the boy. "*Masaahul khair.*"

The boy must have been fourteen. Certainly not any older. He looked clean, apparently not starving. He was rather ruddy on the cheeks, seemingly untouched by the ongoing drama of the war. His inquisitive gaze, initially undefined, became animated with a distinct expression of pleasantness.

Masaahul khair, I had greeted—Arabic for *Good evening.* My accent was rubbish, but it was intelligible enough for him to get what I was up to. And the fact that I spoke any Arabic, however crappy, was the intriguing revelation that suddenly excited the meek boy.

"*Masaahun nur,*" the boy said, as he edged a couple of steps forwards. In the process, he recruited fellow *onlookers* who joined him in marvelling at the oddity of this stranger speaking the language of Prophet Muhammad. Several faces now stared at me when the boy asked, in a cross between Arabic and an irretrievably broken kind of English: "*Amerikiyu?*"

The boy had taken his cue from my shaved head, my pumped-up torso and muscles. It must have given him this inaccurate hint that I was some G.I. in plain clothes. And with his finger conspicuously pointing at me, he suggested somewhat redundantly that his question, was, yes, for me. Briefly, I wondered how he would rather like my answer to be.

Then deciding to find out without delay, I said. "No, I am not an American?"

The boy frowned, and went for another guess. "British?" He still spoke in this accent—the cute cross between Arabic and English.

"No," I smiled. "Not British."

In fact, I was *legally* British, having sworn allegiance to the Queen at that naturalisation ceremony. But I couldn't explain all that to a random urchin in Baghdad.

Now, my answers seemed to confuse the hell out the little man. I had just arrived in the company of *white folks*, speaking English. If I were neither *American* nor *British*, what the hell was I?

Clearly to the boy, it vaguely seemed that it would make no sense for an *African* to have risked life and limb to travel here. Africans—although opposed to the war in their majority—played, at a distance, the part of the *revulsed but safe observer.* Their outrage at the Coalition's actions was indulged from afar.

Now, having run out of options, the boy asked, "*Afriqiu?*"

"Yeah," I confirmed with an observable gush of enthusiasm. "*Afriqiu.*"

The next moment, the boy lurched forth and moved towards me.

He would have freaked me out if his football jersey—featuring *Maradona* in the front—had been bulky above or below to suggest a hidden explosive belt. But he was too lean to be concealing evil. I took the calculated risk of meeting him halfway and stooped slightly to wrap him in an embrace.

"African, good," the boy propounded excitedly as I released him.

I was touched by his innocence and by this unexpected, genuine welcome. *African, good?*

Yeah, I was so touched by his innocence that it began to plague me with one recognisable impulse—a desire to do something.

Years of hosting *lifeline broadcasts*, through which I mediated the reunions of families separated by the Genocide in Rwanda, had nurtured in me the urge to always want to *interfere*. As it were, it didn't take much for me to see one of those many Rwandan kids in this prepubescent boy.

Before my presumptions urged me into some commitment towards the kid, I summoned a determination to guard against developing a rather sudden "Black saviour complex"—one that would have dictated a half-baked plan of flying the boy home to Thamesmead where, I was certain, he would sure have found a room, and two half-sisters. But right when I was primed to cut him loose, the boy wittingly changed the dynamics.

"What your name?" he boy asked in his kindest voice.

I smiled at him. "You could be a good journalist. You ask questions just like one."

He giggled. I couldn't be sure if he understood me well.

"Here's the deal," I continued: "Tell me your name. And I will tell you mine. *Maa ismuk?*"

"*Maa ismuk?*" A couple of voices in the little group reprised my question—*What's your name?*

Oh, yes—my rubbish Arabic. Sure, they made fun of it. But they understood me well enough. And I found this to be pleasant. So, what's the kid's name?

He might have said he was *Azem* or *Hisham*. I satisfied myself with whatever I heard. I settled on *Azem*. Now, it was my turn to hold my end of the bargain.

"*Alhamdulillah*," I said, repressing an urge to laugh. "My name is *Alhamdulillah*."

The little boy and his mates burst into a laughter. *Alhamdulillah?*

No, they couldn't accept this as the possible name of anybody, wherever they might be from—America, Britain, or Africa.

But I wasn't being facetious.

Nshimiyimana, my name, is Kinyarwanda for *Praise Be To God*, for *Hallelujah*. And long before this trip, some Muslim friends had told me that the Islamic mantra, *Alhamdulillah*—often used as a shorthand to signify that *All is well*—literally translates as *Hallelujah*. In other words, *Nshimiyimana* came from a desire of my mother to be praising the Lord every time she called her son.

I made the point to the boy and to his mates, through gestures and performative bad English. And in the end, they got it. How did I know?

After successfully repressing my sudden urge to play "Black Saviour", I figured there was still something I could do to honour my impulse to be of some help. Without much deliberation, my hand found my purse, and I soon parted ways with a few dollar bills—$70, if I remember correctly. Handing the cash to the boy, I intended it as a form of *sadaqah*—a voluntary charitable gift, as prescribed by the Quran, a book that was a big deal in this part of the world. I had left it up to my little friend to decide whether to split the money with the four other members of his makeshift posse.

"You take care my friend," I ultimately called out to the boy.

And as I turned my feet and started for the reception desk, where my heavy items of luggage had now been carted, I heard protracted giggles of contentment. And then: "*Shukram.*" Of course, it was the boy. "*Shukram, Yal Hamdulillah.*"

Those were words of gratitude, addressed with grace to one *Mr. Alhamdulillah*. Yes, he had remembered.

Hallelujah—my little lecture about my name had not been gibberish.

THE BOY WOULDN'T see the flash of contentment that had stayed on my face until the need to address *Reception* turned it off.

That flash?

Well, it was the signature of my satisfaction that just a bit of cash, at the BBC's expense, had made a happy boy out of *Azem*, a little boy whose innocence was being defiled by a war that was beyond his control.

Chapter 21

THE RELOCATION

R unning water in a war zone, even at a five-star hotel, is nothing short of a luxury. I was therefore grateful that there was running water at *The Palestine*. Or at least, in my room. Upon checking in, I rushed into the bathroom to shower away a two-days' accretion of misty grime and fatigue. I had been up for more than 48 hours, and I ached from head to toe.

After shower, I ate a high-protein biscuit and glanced wistfully at the bed. *Not yet*, I told myself. Before I hit the bed to settle my outstanding balance of sleep, I produced my laptop. And for a good ten minutes, I typed away. London had to know what had become of us. The teams in Bush House deserved to be in the loop as to whether they could now begin to fully capitalise on this trip. In a Microsoft Word document, filed under a folder called *The Briefs*, I laid out this draft:

> "Hi all, we made it to Baghdad. In one piece. We were not in the news, so you could have inferred that we are still alive. Anyway, I just checked in, and I'm about to pass out for the night.
>
> Before I do, I'm dropping this quick note to bring you up to date on my position, and to flag up this pitch I think you will love.
>
> Tomorrow, for the afternoon and evening transmissions—as a good scene-setter—I suggest live two-ways on what I'd call a tale of our Passage to Baghdad. Think first-hand witness stuff we saw along the way.
>
> And we did see a great deal: Nasiriyah is in a bad shape; the checkpoints are standing kill zones; and the infamous Highway of Death is not just a lore.
>
> And beyond the obvious tale of death and destruction, I could throw in some general information on the rich history of this country.

And here's how I got the idea: On our way here, we drove through the ancient site of Babylon. While we were there, my homework kicked in and had me thinking Mesopotamia, *and then* Islamic Golden Age.

I would really be happy if what I've been brainstorming on the subject doesn't go to waste. Please, I don't want it to go to waste.

If any of this is of interest, I will send you guys a cue *and a general line of questioning. I'll do that, first thing tomorrow. For now, please, don't try to call. I won't be around to answer—I'll be fast asleep."*

I REVIEWED THE hasty note, and when I determined it contained no set-up for a potential career-ending nightmare, I copied and pasted it in *Outlook*. I hit the *Send* button, then jumped into bed. The bed was surprisingly comfy. There was no reason why it shouldn't have been.

True, I inexplicably anticipated the war to have altered everything—every little experience in this city. But this bed in *The Palestine Hotel* was extravagantly sumptuous. But as to my hopes of *being fast asleep* through the night, I was pitiably mistaken. On my very first night in Bagdad, there was no *being fast asleep*.

Gunfire and explosions—seemingly just yards away

from the hotel—started rumbling sometime before midnight. And as I lay in the bedsheets, listening to the ominous fire festival of rattling tumult, I measured the degree of danger by how much it unsettled my stomach. Sure, it all could have been more impression than reality. But this was a hellish festival. And it rocked on for the best part of what remained of the night.

Those remnants of the Iraqi forces—who had been relatively quiet the last few days—had decided to give us a taste of a real stay in this city under siege. The message conveyed by the sharp cracks of AK-47s and the boomier bangs of light mortar weapons left no doubt that *The Palestine Hotel* had not gone back to being that safe place it once must have been. That message, our security minders got it loud and clear. Suddenly, they wanted no more evidence that leaving us put in this martyred complex could be a stupid mistake.

Were they to take a chance and just hope that these gunfire and explosions, heard this close to the hotel, were merely a one-off that would not repeat in subsequent nights with ultimate, tragic consequences?

With obsessively anxious BBC managers feeding them stern instructions from miles away in London, they were too smart to take such a risk. The *Abrams Tank* deaths still wrapped our wider media fraternity in a lingering cloud of grief. The overbearing reminder of these deaths understandably didn't promote a dalliance with the taking of any kind of credible risk. In fact, our security minders had anticipated everything. They had anticipated this relentless onslaught of gunfire. And what they did next in response would lead to my encounter with the enigmatic woman.

WHATEVER SLEEP I did have in the end belonged not to the night. No, to dare a wink while that unsettling din rattled through the neighbourhood would have qualified as a reckless courtship with death.

I wanted to leave my options wide open. I wanted to hold on to any chance of dodging death if danger waded a path through the night and came all the way to my door. I could afford no such options by falling asleep.

Having spent the last ten hours awake in bed, I was aching from a full night of insomnia when the daybreak arrived at last. The soothing lull, which had come with the morning, reluctantly counselled me to go for a couple hours of snooze. And that, I did at the drop of a hat. I would be ineffective, unable to properly articulate my ideas in the live two-ways, if I braved on, barrelling into a third day with no proper slumber.

When I awoke at 3 p.m.—and what a scandal to have indulged in this over-compensation—the news day across the ocean in London was well under way. And as it appeared, everybody on the afternoon shifts was eager to take up my offer. And that was fine—it was even excellent.

The trouble, however, was that everybody wanted to tailor what was to go into the two-way interviews. Everybody, except the teams at *BBC Great Lakes* and *BBC Focus on Africa*.

At *Focus*, they loved the whole *Passage-To-Baghdad* idea. They also reckoned that a little sprinkle of historical context would add excitement and interest to my first ever reporting from Baghdad. And I wish the whole of Bush House were as accommodating. But how the hell would that be?

"Listen, Venuste, I'm sorry—But we want something from the heart." That was Omar Jumbe. Short, fair of skin, mildly-spoken, polite: Omar was bidding for *BBC Swahili*. "Everything in your pitch," Omar went on, "everything is exciting. I must make this clear, so you don't get me wrong."

Seeing that Omar was being unnecessarily too diplomatic over whatever the real concern was, I chose to free him from his reservations.

"Tell it straight to me, Omar," I urged. "Hey, it's me. Your brother Venuste. You wouldn't play *politician* with me if we were at the *Bush House* lower-ground pub. Why would you do that now? Because I'm in Baghdad?" I laughed. "Speak up!"

Omar laughed along. "Thank you," he said. After a moment of further dithering, he finally decided to talk straight. "Here's the situation: The team would rather you reflect on how the sight of war-related suffering there in Iraq might have stirred up in you some memories from 1994." That was code for the Rwandan Genocide. Omar knew why he had to thread carefully.

"I wouldn't question your collective editorial judgement," I said in a gentle tone, unwilling to be rude in any way. "But the Genocide can't be the main handle into my first reporting from the field about this Iraqi tragedy. Omar, Iraq is easily the story of the decade, if not the century. It stands on its own."

After a confused moment of silence, Omar asked: "What do you mean?"

"You heard me," I called out respectfully. I was still mindful not to come across as condescending to Omar. If anything, Omar was just a messenger. "Say, your show is later picked up for a random BBC programme review. You'd be savagely berated for being editorially erratic. You can't possibly think that the BBC sent me here to reflect on 1994, while we have everything of a humanitarian disaster unfolding right now under our nose. Think about it, Omar."

Omar gave himself a couple of seconds to think. Before his silence became uncomfortable, he resumed, remaining calm but insistent. "Sorry, Venuste," he said. "I'd be glad to defend our reasoning at any BBC programme review. We are BBC Africa. We want you to take this closer home. Let's not over-think it."

I was losing the argument. And Omar could sense it all. "Can you do this?" he pressed. "I don't mean to be a pain."

But he was being a pain.

Anyway, I could do what was being requested. I just didn't want to do it. For two reasons.

First, talking about the Genocide was always a tearjerker for me. To put it bluntly, it messes me up. And second, from the piles of rubble in Baghdad here, talking of 1994 seemed to be a gallop away from the actual story at hand. I sincerely thought it was far-fetched.

Yes, I agree the Genocide was a tragedy so horrific that Africa; that the world wasn't about to forget. But making a major storyline of it on my first day reporting from Baghdad seemed editorially unsound.

However, Omar was a nice colleague. If anything, he knew not to speak to anyone but gently. The fine character of Omar was weighing more heavily in his favour than the collective editorial judgement of his team. And as it were, I soon relented. And while I now prayed God for this never to ultimately happen, for whatever convenient reason, I told Omar, "Yes, this sure is something I can do."

Omar Jumbe, happy to have won for *BBC Swahili*, laughed out his relief.

"Certainly, you can do this," he said.

I didn't laugh when I responded, "Let me get back to you."

And as gently as Omar spoke, I ended the call and moved on to deal with a real torpedo; one in flesh and blood. And that torpedo was a *Mr. Idriss*

Abassou, the Planning Editor of *BBC French*, a truly unpleasant character.

In reading that email from Abassou, I had gathered he was exceedingly cross at me for a complete host of reasons. He particularly accused me of being lazy. In his book of damnation, I was guilty of being too cautious. And my specific sin was to have been proposing a safe and easy two-way on some *Passage To Baghdad*, whereas I could do better. Was I not already in town? What prevented me from getting the hell out to some real place in the city, talk to good and bad Iraqis, and then do a real live two-way from there?

"You are asking me right now to do everything against the book," I complained to Abassou, now that I had him on the phone. "We just got in town. We have not even had a chance to get our bearings, and assess security. This is a war zone if I shall remind you."

"Frankly," Idriss interrupted, "that's your problem. You could have turned this assignment down. Instead, you agreed to it. And I am now just asking you to do what you are there for—work."

Right there, I lost my temper.

"What have you got against me?" I attacked. "You wanted this duty trip? Why didn't you put up your hand? Why did you not bid for it?"

Cornered, the Planning Editor moved on to a different type of recrimination, but I now barely listened. And he had been going on about it when some knuckles came hard against the door of the hotel room. Someone had come along. And they were knocking with urgency.

WHILE I WOULD probably not have enjoyed the disturbance under another set of circumstances, I welcomed the knock with a rush of hope. With no heads-up, I put Abassou on hold, and made it for the door. When I pulled it open, I was overtaken by what I saw.

Instead of a member of the hotel staff as I half-expected, there stood a bearish silhouette with a crestfallen face.

"Richard?" I called.

And *Richard Blunt*, our Field Team Leader, took a step forward into the room, knocking me aside. He was super unhappy. And I could only guess it all had to do with me. But how exactly?

"Richard," I tried again. "What's up?"

"No," Richard barked. "I must ask you that."

As the Team Leader thus bellowed angrily, a bushy frown rode over his heavy brows. And he spoke in that crisp accent. I mean, it was none of the *post-code Cockney stuff*. Richard meant business.

"I didn't sleep well," I said. "And I am not good at riddles."

Richard's bushy eyebrows swayed. "Venuste, this is no proper conduct," he blamed. "Every fucking body is waiting downstairs at the lobby. We'd have been gone now if you weren't holding us back."

"Gone," I asked, a lot confused. "Where?"

"Do you check your emails?" Richard's bushy brow was in flux again—a millipede in rapid motion. "And the memo I left for each of you guys at Reception?"

Oh, I could see the problem.

I had a lot of unread emails. Including any that Richard might have sent. And my priorities, since waking up, didn't include taking a stroll downstairs to Reception.

Lowering my head in resignation, I looked askance at the *Nokia* in my hand, drawing Richard's attention to it. "I had a rough night. Just woke up a little over an hour ago. And since, I have been trying to keep the teams at Bush House from rioting."

Richard glared. "Not your bloody team, again—" He stopped sharply. And his eyes widened in incremental realisation, as though he was afraid someone who should not, might have heard his cursing. He slowly pointed at the cell phone in my hand and whispered. "Is whoever *that is* still on the line?"

Yes, Idriss Abassou—the Planning Editor—was still there. "I'm afraid so," I said.

Richard did something that showed he was seriously pissed: Lurching forward, he snatched the *Nokia*, and blurted into it, "Can you guys back off a second? We file when we are bloody ready to." The Team Leader rammed a finger into a key, disconnecting the call.

It was out of character. And as a bewildered witness to this instant insanity, I asked, "What's going on?"

Richard stared. "Were you dead last night? You heard the gunfire?"

No, I wasn't dead last night. And yes, I heard the bloody gunfire. And I made sure Richard didn't ask me this question again.

"So, why do you think it's reasonable to drag our feet as we relocate out of this goddamn place?"

I didn't think anything of that at all. And while I was tempted to protest like a disagreeable devil, I made the choice to focus. "Are we relocating?" I asked.

Richard just sulked.

His dismissive cold shoulder made me feel clueless and stupid on the spot. But I would soon thank the Team Leader for ever knocking so urgently at that door.

Not only had he rescued me from the unbearable burns of Idriss Abassou, also it took his banging and our subsequent hasty exit from *The Palestine Hotel* to set up my encounter with the enigmatic woman

Shahida—that was the name of the woman. But to me, she was Scheherazade. For like her namesake in *The Arabian Nights*, she was a captivating storyteller; one with understandable mood swings, which made her even more interesting.

Thank you, Richard.

Thanks for that nuisance.

PART IV

THIS FALLEN CITY

Each day had the same bloody rhythm: mortars at dawn, car bombs by 11:00 a.m., drive-by shootings before tea, and mortars again at dusk. At night the death squads went to work.

—RICHARD ENGEL
And Then All Hell Broke Loose

Chapter 22

STAYING THE COURSE

The first week of residency in the fortified villa opposite the vacated French Embassy—a short stroll from the *Palestine Hotel*—was agonisingly slow, dragging on like a long chain of Victorian wagons drawn by a moody snail. Or so it felt to me. But what was the reality?

Under the onslaught of the many storylines to pursue, I drowned in a hyper-awareness that I had no alternative but to deliver. I felt that I couldn't afford to make a mistake, not for my own sake, but for the sake of the woman who had placed her trust in me. I owed it to Kari Blackburn not to hand over any ammunition to her hidden or manifest in-house rivals. To put it more bluntly, this assignment had become more about her than it had any right to be. How could she retain any confidence to vouch for Black Africans on future major BBC assignments if I screwed this up? And wouldn't I be blowing it for anyone younger within the BBC who fitted my demographics if this special assignment went south?

Evidently, white colleagues of *Team BBC* in Baghdad might have been anguishing under concerns of their own. But unlike me, they were not mentally punished by a nagging sense that the future chances of staff members who shared their unimpeachable characteristics depended on how well they did in their coverage of this war. While my colleagues found it easier to unwind, I remained perpetually wound tight.

Let's consider, for instance, a birthday celebration held in a sheltered venue for one of our female colleagues. Given the circumstances, I had the uneasy sense that it was somewhat inappropriate. Amidst the music and booze, war reporters mingled with soldiers seeking momentary respite, and a few revellers were carefree enough to engage in rough, improvised sexual encounters against a wall in a barely secluded corner. I couldn't help but wonder how they could focus on such matters amidst the prevailing chaos in town.

But if I was that sanctimonious, what the hell was I doing there?

Well, I attended the party spontaneously, without any premeditation, and somehow ended up making it about work. Truth is, I had genuinely hoped to take advantage of this moment of carefree abandon to relax a bit. Yet, with my mind preoccupied by the violence of the conflict, and the evidence I had seen of it, I remained completely immune to the sense of enjoyment that surrounded me. I gloomily lingered on the outskirts of the party, biding my time until a wonderful opportunity arose. And that's when a British Army officer approached me.

Spotting me in my aloneness amid the crowd, the officer had become curious. He pulled up and levelled with me for a chat. I expected it all to be some inane banter, as would suit a boozy birthday party. But it turned quickly into a story in the making.

The fellow seemed too wet—stoned to a good degree—that he never knew he was lowering his guard. With no filter on, he settled on discussing the turn *Operation Iraqi Freedom* was about to take. Apparently, a *nasty storm* was brewing away from the capital. And for a reason only known to him, he wanted a journalist to know about it.

For his opening gambit, as he determined to *unload* his insight on me, he bluntly accused, "You journalists are having the wool pulled over your eyes." His voice was fairly audible above the din of the birthday party And what a hell of a start! Surely, if he had intended to pique my interest with his quip, it was instant success.

Repressing my eagerness, I asked, "What are you trying to tell me? *We are having the wool pulled over our eyes?*"

"I'll bet my last penny that you are," the officer

affirmed. "This country is about to explode under your nose, and you don't even seem to realise it—you are here having fun."

"How's that so?" I asked.

"There's a storm brewing in the *Anbar* Province," the man clarified immediately, slightly straightening up, widening the gap between us. "Saddam's folks in that area have been duplicitous from the start. Now, they are about to give us a run for our money."

Wow.

He had already given me the basic foundation for my story. Pushing for a little more of details—which I could flesh out with a backstory search in the BBC private archives—I said, "Where exactly in the Anbar Province is this trouble cooking up?"

"One thing, first," he said, ready to demonstrate that he wasn't that stoned after all. In the dim lights of the party venue, he now glared suspiciously at me. "I never told you my name, did I?"

I took a second to understand what he meant.

"No, never," I said reassuringly. "You never told me your name."

And that was true. But the captain's name was visible on his fatigues for he was not dressed for a party. Even for this birthday, they had come ready for combat.

"If there's a worthy story in this," I clarified, "the *anonymous BBC source* would be a vague British Army officer. So, you never told me your name."

The stranger nodded his satisfaction. "Ramadi,

Fallujah," he said. "These are time bombs." There, he paused to wander a look around the room, and with apparent concern, he studied the happy crowd in the dim light of the bunker. "Some of these young men," he continued, alluding to the servicemen in the room, "some of them may be attending their very last party ever."

That made me sad. Instinctively, I asked, "Why?"

"Don't be this naive," he snorted. "We have not just been killing them. They are killing us, too. Oh, I see you haven't made it yet anywhere near the airfields where we load up the coffins back to Britain and America."

He was right. And I said nothing.

"Not your fault," he excused me. "You won't be allowed near our dead colleagues. But perhaps, you can easily admit the concept that no one engaged in this stupid war is safe."

The stranger spoke some more, and then said something to suggest he was done with our impromptu chat. Though I believed he had said enough and that I should now warmly thank him, I held him back. "*Mission accomplished*," I said. "Is it not?"

He smiled sourly. It was an indication that he understood my reference to Bush's triumphant announcement from weeks earlier. And before he articulated the meaning of his sour smile, he seemed to regret something. It was as though he had just realised that journalists—whether born and bred in Kigali or in Kilburn—are never any safe chatting partners. They seemed to never seriously engage in conversations, except with the ulterior motive of getting you to *defenestrate* yourself by saying more than you should. Well, I was just speculating. He never told me he was conflicted in any way.

"I didn't give you my name," the man said again with insistence, a subtle reminder that I may quote him if I would, but only on condition of anonymity. "Now, either from Bush or from me, never take what you are told at face value. Apparently, you journalists out here have not been doing a good job of that."

That was a subtle dig. *What do I say?*

Before I could comment, the stranger raised a knowing eyebrow and with a stiff nod, he said, "Loosen up, friend. You must not forget to enjoy the party. And good luck." Then, he disappeared into a corner of this place overrun by carefree thrill seekers.

Immediately afterwards, I began to compose in my head the email I was to send back to Bush House, pitching a *two-way* on the "brewing trouble" in *Anbar*. A quick search through the ENPS system into the BBC's intranet archives unearthed enough for my pitch to stick. And when I went on-air the next evening on *Focus*, I dutifully granted the officer the anonymity he requested.

UNDER THE OPPRESSION of my *self-inflicted pressure to perform*, my sense of time became warped. The span of each day appeared exceedingly lengthy enough that any of my potential worst nightmares seemed to have all the time necessary to materialise. But I was determined for that never to happen. So, I ruthlessly held my head down and pursued those storylines, and kept filing *stuff* through the *ISDN* box to London.

And my stories were a mix of a great deal.

The calm desperation of Sergio Vieira de Melo—the UN Special Representative for Iraq—telling me in perfect French, months before he was slain in a truck bomb, that *Iraq was an unprecedented man-made humanitarian crisis*; the pent-up fury of that small crowd in Sadr City, swarming around my microphone outside the mosque after the Friday prayer, impatient at the Americans, eager to swear that Saddam Hussein was so treacherous that he couldn't have been done yet; the lament of the wife and mother whose husband—a journalist, as my Iraqi fixers were told—had been railroaded out and into some yet-unidentified prison. His world had thus shifted after a squad of American soldiers, hunting for diehard Fedayeen fighters, ran down his family home.

From one day to another, my stories—and the people they portrayed—looked quite different. But there was a recurring centrepiece. And it was my quasi-obsession about the 24/7 American military patrols in the streets of Baghdad.

The military patrols were an eyesore. I was diligent to inject into my daily *two-ways* that none of the unwieldy *M1 Abrams* Tanks, the armoured Humvees and Stryker vehicles, the Bradley fighting vehicles: none suggested anything but a siege. Whenever I was given more time on-air than I had fresh news to fill it with, I almost made it an art form to rehash—as though in a stump speech—that *Saddam Hussein is gone, but the country he once ruled with an iron fist is far from having been liberated.*

That, of course, sounded like opinion. But it was nothing but an observable fact. Baghdad teemed with so many American military engines that the *fallen city* looked like a loose and vast, open-sky version of an American military camp.

As I pursued those storylines, and was on a streak filing to London, something amazing happened—an unexpected stream of praises. For a variety of reasons.

"*Consummate professionalism,*" according to one *BBC Africa* Senior Editor who was proud that an "asset of our own" was putting the Regional Editorial Hub on the wider map of the BBC. *Anecdotal*, I thought. But I took the compliment with grace.

"*Your human-interest reporting exposes a very unsettling side of this war,*" another satisfied party pontificated with too much panache. Then, this gushing line from a manager's email: "*What a terrific display of linguistic mastery!*"

It was heart-warming, to say the least. But the most consequential of it all was what the formidable Kari Blackburn had to say.

WE WERE A few days short of the third week of our mission when Kari Blackburn got on the phone to me. The call was part of her routine performance of the BBC's duty of care. But with Kari, it was always more than just performative.

"How's *Team BBC* doing there?" she had said when I picked her call.

In the face of it, her question was a simple one. But not quite so in reality.

One thing unknown to Kari was that *Team BBC* counted at least an extra member—*Shahida*, the enigma also known to me as *Scheherazade*. I had not cleared with Management the *creep mission* I had allowed her to embark on. She was meant to be just *The Landlady*.

But I could not just stand to see her indigenous knowledge of Baghdad and its people go to waste. *Scheherazade* quietly became more than the *landlady*.

She became a lot of things—cultural consultant, driver, cook, *super fixer*. And when circumstances required it, she delegated the *fixing tasks* to three rough and reliable young men, whose Arabic language skills, and whose knowledge of the lay of the land, made more than half of my stories possible.

I am ashamed to say this—Apart from the small fees they were paid for their diligence, *Asif, Imru'* and *Khaleed* were never given credit on-air when I signed off a despatch or a *two-way*. They never asked for more than the few dollars in fixing fees; they never cared for on-air credit.

Asif, *Imru'* and *Khaleed* were beautifully full of gratitude for the opportunity to monetise their skills amid the chaos of war. At my own discretion, I had chosen to withhold disclosure of *Scheherazade*'s role as *commander-in-chief* of my little army of *fixers*.

At any rate, I enjoyed the company of these dutiful young men. And this is one interesting thing about their lovely lot: They staunchly believed in *Maktub*, or the *Qadr*, or divine destiny. Unlike our bunch who attended bootcamps before showing up in town, they were not given that choice. This was their country and violence had come uninvited. They had to live through it. And unlike our bunch, they didn't worry a lot about death.

I should confess that I saw something very *African* in their stoic approach to life. Without ever knowing them from a previous life, I understood them straight away. And I agreed with *The Landlady* that to deny these fixers my business on the account of Western standards of safety and security would have had a side of ironic cruelty to it. Even away from me, they would only be without a job. But they weren't any safer. This was Baghdad.

As it happened, no higher-up at the BBC were to know that I had made an exception for my use of the good young fellows. I did not refer up. And it had rather served my reporting exceedingly well.

Now, what was I to tell Kari Blackburn who was enquiring about *Team BBC*? Should she know about my *shadow army* of fixers? Should she know that *The Landlady* was more than a *landlady*?

No, I decided to leave the Boss out of the loop. For her own good. If push comes to shove, she must be able to argue, with full integrity, that she did not know I was being *proactive* beyond a certain limit. Kari must not know that I had allowed the terrain to dictate my manoeuvres rather than the manual, the rule book. So, I told Kari just what she ought to know.

I told Kari that *Team BBC* was operating just fine. Which was true.

We shared stories, clips, perspectives, corned beef. We traded jokes when we could afford a downtime, as we rarely did. At the villa, I *bunked* with Stephen Sackur. And very funnily enough, Stephen—who mistakenly thought I was the youngest of the team—was dutifully *territorial* in looking out for me. He wanted me safe. And if there wasn't enough of anything to go round— water, bread, beef briskets—he made a case for me to be served first. In return, if I were to inform no one at all about my sneaky movements by day or night, I still had to keep Stephen in the loop. Yes, *Team BBC* was a close-knit family in more than a way.

But on-air, of course, it was down to every individual reporter to put up their best performance. If only because the by-line was not a collective thing. The by-line at the end of each report could only be *personal*, as could any later eventual accolades.

Having made my mind to mince what to report, I

gladly told Kari Blackburn: "Our team is out of this world; it's the best team I have ever been part of."

"I wouldn't say I know you to be prone to exaggerations," Kari laughed. "I can only be glad to hear that all is well."

"I'm certainly not exaggerating," I reassured, only vaguely guilty that I could not tell her about my *shadow fixers*. "Everything's really fine here. We are supportive of each other. Unless you've heard something to the contrary. Any complaint against me from the teams?" Here, I vaguely had Idriss Abassou in mind.

Kari made a dismissive *huff*. "Oh, not at all. In fact, you may be very pleased to know that we are all happy here with your work."

"Are you, Boss?" I asked sceptically.

"Why should we not be?" the boss replied. "There's even better, Venuste. I hear that you've made it hard for all the *Jeremiahs* at *BBC French* to get mighty high on their horses about your case." She giggled.

And I found it funny the way she creatively used the word *Jeremiahs*.

Wrapping up the call, Kari continued, "The best response to any criticism—constructive or otherwise—is to let your work do the talking. I am very proud of you. Naturally, there will be a time to *properly* say *thank you*. For now, just do more of the same. But keep safe—If you can't report it safely, forget about it. But, of course, I'm preaching here to the choir."

IT WAS A short call, and while it may seem like an exaggeration, Kari Blackburn's words marked a turning point in my assignment. They created a clear distinction between the time *before* and the time *after* that moment: From feeling awkward with a sense that I had everything to prove, I suddenly became imbued with such a mental strength. It made me question why I ever doubted myself in the first place. As a result of my accrued strength, I developed greater ambitions. Now, I wanted the desperate hunt for those *Weapons of Mass Destruction* to turn up something, so that I could don my gas mask, run over there to report on the eventual find in the full spectrum of these four *BBC Broadcast languages* that I commanded. Oh God, I now felt strong, powerful.

Deep down, however, I thought my assignment could not get any more exciting. But I was wrong. As I was soon to find out. And when I did, even the wonderful Kari Blackburn would drag her feet. Even Kari Blackburn would find herself at a loss as to how best she could tactfully get me to back the hell off.

Chapter 23

THE FRENCH CONNECTION

When the terrorists struck on *September 11*, France responded with the unwavering support of a close friend and ally. The national outpouring of solidarity was captured soberly by the front page of *Le Monde* on the following day: "*Nous sommes tous américains.*" In ordinary times, that would have been the unlikeliest statement to slip off a French tongue. The French proudly thought of themselves as many *things*, and *American* was never one of those. Tragedy, however, forces one to re-examine their standing perspectives.

Within a week of the attacks—as soon as the skies reopened to traffic—French President Jacques Chirac flew across the Atlantic and became the first foreign leader to meet with George Bush in the wake of the tragedy. The picture of a grim-faced Chirac by the window of a helicopter surveying *Ground Zero* in New York would become emblematic of France's solidarity. And though a picture is worth a thousand words, Chirac—ever the wordsmith—still had to back up the compelling imagery with *words*.

Waxing lyrical to reporters before getting down to business with President Bush, the Frenchman spoke of himself as a messenger tasked with conveying to America a *solidarity of the heart* from the French people.

"We are completely determined to fight by your side this new type of evil, of absolute evil, which is terrorism," Chirac pledged. "France is prepared and available to discuss all means to fight and eradicate this evil."

This was long before *French fries* in America defiantly became *Freedom fries*. But even then, the first snowflakes of the upcoming frost between Paris and Washington already floated in the air. While a confident President Bush praised his guest as a *man of vision* and looked forward to France's help in waging what he called a *new kind of war*, he was brought up sharply over his choice of words.

"I don't know if we should use the word *war*," Chirac protested carefully. "Now, we are faced with a conflict of a completely new nature; a conflict that is attempting to destroy human rights, freedom, the dignity of man, and I believe that everything must be done to safeguard these values of civilisation."

After meeting with UN Secretary General Kofi Annan in New York, Chirac's position on the appropriate response to the *"absolute evil of terrorism"* had solidified into one of a greater caution. He no longer spoke of France as *completely determined to fight by the side* of America, but as *only willing to participate, in agreement with other European and global partners.* In other words, France could unconditionally share America's pain, but found it unreasonable to subscribe blindly to any retaliatory folly.

Of course, at the time of Chirac's visit, the US-led invasion of Iraq was still two years away, but the two allies were already drifting apart and fast.

In the late winter of 2003, the solidarity trip seemed all but forgotten when France lead Germany— among other countries—in a rather resounding opposition to the War.

And when the UN Security Council met to vote on the use of force against Saddam Hussein, France's Foreign Minister, Dominique de Villepin, would leave America red in the face by laying into the Bush Administration's eagerness to forsake the way of peaceful resolution in favour of violence.

"No one can assert that the path of war will be shorter than that of the inspections," de Villepin submitted to the Council, earning himself some cheers from his audience. "No one can claim either that it might lead to a safer, more just and more stable world."

FROM ACROSS THE ocean, my wife had patiently held off her scepticism and allowed me to talk at length about the French and their legendary passionate opposition to the war. It was our first proper natter in days. Amid the demands of travel and the intensity of duty, we couldn't keep the promise of our nightly telephone catch-ups. But now that I had nothing to prove, seeing that everybody who mattered at Bush House was all up in praise of my work, I thought I could relax a bit. So, I did and called home.

It was early evening in Baghdad when I eagerly rang her. We had a lot to review, including our hasty exit from the *Palestine Hotel*. Dedeli had raised this particular issue, with the concern of a wife who felt left out of a crucial decision.

"If the Palestine Hotel isn't safe enough for you," she had said, "what makes your villa any safer?"

"The villa is opposite the French Embassy," I said.

My wife's expression—as I read in her sudden shift of pitch—hardened. "But why the French Embassy?" she challenged. "Why not the German Embassy? Or any other embassy?"

I now felt a pang of guilt for leaving Dedeli out of the loop.

"Listen," I said rather tensely, "as far as the BBC security advisers are concerned, the vicinity of the French Embassy is closer to the most neutral territory you can have in Baghdad."

She kissed her teeth, which she almost never did.

"What does that mean? I often wonder what you are talking about."

Clearly, we weren't making the most of this catch-up. I started to feel impatient with the way things were going. But I knew that expressing my frustration would only make things worse.

I took a deep breath to calm down.

"George Bush might have a strong dislike for Jacques Chirac," I said, "but he is not likely to order a missile strike on *the area.*"

"You can't be so sure," Dedeli sneered.

"Yes, I can," I challenged. "France has yet to re-establish full diplomatic ties with Iraq since the first Gulf War in 1991. And considering that any French official of whatever rank who had remained in Baghdad must have left before the *Shock-And-Awe* Campaign, an American strike against the place would be the most pointless thing to do, even for someone as slow as President Bush."

Dedeli loved to chime in whenever I took a swipe at Bush, the hawkish commander-in-chief. But now, she stayed silent.

In her silence, she struggled to accept that the grounds for our exit from the *Palestine Hotel* were any sound. While it was unlikely that the Americans would shoot at an embassy, even that of France, my wife was concerned about other threats in Baghdad. And she was right, of course. As she pointedly argued, any remaining fighters loyal to Saddam could mount an assault in the area, and then blame it on the Coalition, if not simply to display their rage at the Western media, of which I was part and parcel.

"It's a decent hypothesis," I told her. "But it's just hard to see any fighter loyal to Saddam turning up here for trouble. It's really hard."

To convince my wife once and for all, before I heard the expected knock at the door, I took her all the way up to September 2001, up to President Chirac's American solidarity trip. Then, I recounted to her the chain of events, highlighting the reason why *French fries* had become *Freedom Fries*.

Ultimately, I came to rest my argument on that showdown in the chamber of the Security Council where De Villepin prosaically rose supreme in the name of his country to assume the moral high ground over America on what he had framed as an *ideal, a conscience of which the UN was a keeper.*

"The Baathist regime might have fallen apart," I said at last. "The French might have failed to prevail in their opposition to the war. But if any fighters loyal to Saddam cannot celebrate France for taking their side in opposing America, they wouldn't mount an attack against any French interest in this country. At least, this is the reasoning of the security experts who wanted us out of the *Palestine.*"

Dedeli was in no rush to deliver her final words. She knew her silent breaks were just as meaningful as her most passionate submissions. And by her penultimate recourse to silence, I sensed an unspoken vehement rejection of what was nothing but sophisticated bullshit to her. Because of that nag in her head, my wife had not enjoyed this natter at all. The girls almost never featured in it, which was highly unusual.

After the long pause, she said, "If you say it's safer there in your villa than at the *Palestine*, good for you. But something doesn't add up. I just hope you're not hiding anything important from me."

That early evening—if I knew what I now know—I would have marvelled, more than ever, at the unique power of Dedeli's sense of intuition.

Chapter 24

THE SCHEHERAZADE
CONUNDRUM

The Landlady arrived moments after Dedeli hung up. She proceeded into the dining area of the ensuite, and there she lowered herself into a chair. I had trailed her closely. Now, I was enthroned in an armchair across from her. Without any vanity, I must observe that *Scheherazade* was a woman of grace and beauty. She reminded me of that fact wherever we first met in the day.

This evening, she was dressed in creamy cashmere slacks, and her well-tended jet-black hair flowed freely down her neck. She appeared to me, now more than ever, a perfect fit of how she described herself—a modern Muslim woman. I wondered why she would ever feel the need to inform anyone of the obvious. Back in the Baghdad of the Caliphate, she might not even have been entitled to oversee this secluded piece of real estate, half-hidden here behind these high walls of concrete and palm trees. But better than mere care-taking, the woman owned the whole thing.

"Let me address an element of a cultural importance," *Scheherazade* said, speaking a flawless English, in an accent that carried a light tincture of her native Arabic. "While staying among the Arabs, if you are not invited home to share a family meal, you are yet just another stranger."

Uncertain, I said, "You're clearly making an interesting point."

Scheherazade looked up, as though to inspect the ceiling for spots that might need mending. But the ceiling was spotless.

"In the last three weeks," she continued, "I have heard more about Africa and the Rwandan people than ever before in my entire life. As a result, you are now both a stranger and not quite one anymore. I didn't bring dinner. I want you to dine at home."

Upon hearing this clarification, I felt deeply moved. "This is truly heartening to hear, *Shahida*," I said sincerely. "Certainly, yes—I would be delighted to partake in some full Arab hospitality."

Smiling, the landlord gently gestured with her palm, which was strikingly smooth. "But I am not done," she said. "This is not a date."

I glanced at her. She met my gaze and lowered hers, smiling.

"I am a married Muslim woman," she added. "In this part of the world, it's more than just a marital status. It's a lot of things."

I found her directness refreshing. But any risk of crossing a line here was nil. I was in awe of this mystery the landlady had about herself. Otherwise, I felt nothing akin to lust for her. Furthermore, Baghdad at this time of war was the wrong place to pick if I were ever tempted to transgress the Lord's *Commandments*.

"As a married *Christian* man, myself," I stated, "I feel very safe knowing that your *grace* is strict about her moral boundaries. Our world needs more people of your kind, Shahida."

"Thank you," she beamed, and added: "There's one last thing, my friend."

"Let me guess," I laughed. "There's no ham on the menu."

Perhaps busy with what to say next, she failed to get my joke.

Setting aside any jesting, I inquired, "One last thing? What is it?"

She responded with a serious tone, "I need your opinion on a matter, but you must promise not to breathe a word of it to the white boy."

The white boy? She was undoubtedly referring to Stephen Sackur, my roommate.

Like most evenings, Stephen was out at his usual spot—the Al-Rasheed Hotel. As usual, I had the ensuite all to myself.

With a playful lean-in, driven by sudden curiosity, I theatrically whispered, "Are we hatching a plan against the *white boy*?" I chuckled, aiming to keep the atmosphere light. "Remember, it's my duty to watch over him here. No plotting, please."

"Plotting?" Scheherazade's voice carried a hint of disgust. "No, God forbid. It's just that I find it hard to trust white people." She gave me a brief, direct stare. "Especially considering they are the ones destroying my country. My friend, this war is a heartless violation against us and our people. Is it inhumane to be wary of those who are responsible for the loss of your loved ones?"

The intensity of her words caught me off guard. Until now, Scheherazade had concealed, behind an inscrutable veil, her true feelings about the invasion. She had diverted our discussions with unrelated stories, seemingly avoiding the topic altogether. But in that moment, she briefly laid bare her genuine emotions, only to retreat into herself, apparently overwhelmed by regret. Perhaps, she questioned if I were deserving of her trust. Perhaps, she was horrified by her own vulnerability, mortified over the breach of her practiced fortitude.

Regardless, she appeared as though she wished to retract what she had just revealed. And as I sensed her *unease*, I decided to *ease* the tension.

"You don't trust white people?" I asked cautiously, with a gentle smile.

I wanted to ensure she didn't feel judged, as that could cause her to withdraw.

"I don't trust them," she replied, her tone oozing with calm defiance.

"Well," I responded, "you should know that you're not alone. Black people share that sentiment, too. Remember *slavery* and stuff?"

As if following a script, both of us burst into laughter, and for a while the room resounded with our shared amusement.

After a moment, as the tearoom settled into a quieter atmosphere, I reassured Scheherazade, "I am more than willing to be your confidant. I won't utter a word to the white boy."

IN THE POST-APOCALYPTIC scenes of some Hollywood movies, there was often a brutal, heartless villain who went on living bountifully, even eating delicacies, and drinking fine wines out of some well-hidden hideout amidst the rubble of what had once been human civilisation. At the dinner table, I couldn't shake the picture of Scheherazade as that Hollywood odd villain, not on the account of any credible wickedness, but because of her apparent dexterity at surviving luxuriously.

The woman had been a mystery to me since day one. From the get-go, I suspected she was a Baathist, one that must have, perhaps, been flipped by the CIA sometime during its pre-invasion covert manoeuvres.

That assumption, however, now lay in tatters, considering her angry outburst at the *untrustworthy white invaders*. But even if she were a foreign asset, could that have been anything as nefarious as, say, *bodysnatching*?

No, if Scheherazade were malevolent, she could not have been more so than anyone who just had enough sense to bail out of a sinking ship.

Over sour tea, after a dinner of lamb roast and bread, the woman surprised me with her chosen topic of discussion.

"Saddam Hussein was still here in town when the Americans arrived," she said.

I was shocked, but I didn't challenge her. I wanted to keep her talking.

"How did he elude capture?" I asked. "Did he not leave before the storming of the Airport?"

Scheherazade adamantly shook her head. "Saddam was still here in Baghdad on 9th April," she affirmed, referring to the very day the Coalition took control of the Iraqi Capital. "He left after the *Zuhr* prayer," the landlady continued. "He had earlier met with a loyalist circle of Baath members whom he ordered to resist. He then prayed and left, hiding in an unmarked three-car convoy."

This disclosure was too much to process. It left me with a stampede of questions.

Can this be true?

Why is she telling me this?

Is this her way of confessing indirectly that my suspicions about her were right? Was she telling me she belonged to that loyal circle of Baath members?

The tea being too sour for my taste, I had long given it up and was now lost in my inner dialogue.

Then, Scheherazade asked, "What do you think of the BBC?"

Further intrigued by her fresh query, I wondered what exactly I should not share with Stephen: the seemingly ludicrous claim about Saddam or the incipient discussion about the BBC?

Perhaps it's both, I thought.

"What do you think of the BBC?" she repeated

I stared at her. "What do you mean?"

Wearing a serious air, Scheherazade clarified. "Does the truth matter to the BBC? Forget just for a moment that you are part of the organisation. Is the BBC anything more than a Western propaganda machine?"

Struggling to see the point of the question, while wondering whether there could possibly be any ethical answer to it, I went for a copout. I asked her, "What do you think of the BBC?"

Scheherazade scoffed as though her answer was supposed to be obvious.

"Britain and America are the invaders," she said. "The role of British and American soldiers is to point and shoot and drop bombs. What's the role here of the British and American media outlets? Cheer them on?"

Baffled, I said vaguely, "This is a good question."

The landlady nodded. "And a simple one. So, tell me: Does the *British Broadcasting Corporation* care about the truth?"

I carefully considered Scheherazade's logic. I did so for a while.

"Tony Blair and his Cabinet might support this war," I said at last, "but the majority of the British people are against it. As a publicly-funded organisation, the BBC owes the truth to the people. The BBC is certainly not accountable to Tony Blair."

She sneered. "If only this were true."

"It's true," I said.

"I find it hard to believe."

Noting the sadness that had crept into her voice, I indirectly offered some sympathy.

"I understand your position," I told her. "But you are not getting a more honest coverage of this war from any other media outlet. The BBC's reporting of the war is the closest to the truth that you will ever get. And I speak as an *African* with insider's knowledge."

Scheherazade drew a long sigh and blinked slowly at me. Whatever she had to say next seemed stuck in her.

In the hope of coaxing her into overcoming her inner block, I asked, "Is this the stuff you want me to keep from the white boy?"

She chuckled, then rubbed her beautiful eyes with her smooth palms. When she finally fixed that familiar clear stare on me and spoke again, I was stunned.

"Would you," she said, "interview Saddam Hussein for the British Broadcasting Corporation?"

THIS IS ONE thing about us, journalists—we are sceptics by professional deformation, but we believe that what's too good to be true can sometimes be true, indeed. One just doesn't want to spend the rest of a lifetime regretting the loss of a major story because of over-cautiousness. And for that, we quickly learn to come to terms with the occasional wild goose chase.

An interview with Saddam Hussein, the current World's number-one fugitive? It required a leap of faith. And why the hell not?

When my initial shock finally subsided and I vetoed my inner sceptic to accept that I possibly stood on the cusp of the biggest opportunity of my career, I found myself staring at a narrow window for action.

As it happened next, I was in a race against time when I intruded into the peaceful Sunday of Kari Blackburn in London, seeking urgent guidance while disclosing very little.

Chapter 25

STAND IT DOWN

It wasn't about the delicate ethics of whose side we ultimately stood on, as British Broadcasting Corporation. Undoubtedly, the glaring ethical question was whether it was editorially sound to extend the agony of a brutal regime by giving it an opportunity for more propaganda. But the deciding factor was safety, security. Why ever could I think of violating everything I was taught at bootcamp to consider such a reckless idea? When had it suddenly become fine to attempt the pursuit of a story at the risk of life and limb?

If only because Kari Blackburn wanted me back home in one piece to my daughters whom she had once met at Bush House, her move to exercise veto power must have been her automatic response.

But her logic for doing so was compelling.

Every American and British soldier out there across the country; every former dissident whose time seemed to have now come for prominence and revenge; every professional or amateur bounty hunter: everyone—except my shadowy go-between—would do anything to find out where the hell Saddam *the bloody* Hussein was hiding. Did I happen to think that an American fighter jet pilot would hesitate to fire if they picked my signals and triangulated me to the location wherever the interview would take place?

"The brief was clear," Kari reminded. "You are not there on a suicide mission."

The Boss had taken the rest of Sunday to think, and most of Monday to consult with her superiors. Then on Tuesday at around 2:00 p.m., she called to give me her unvarnished verdict.

I had listened quietly, like a good boy.

"Let's get back to our senses," she pleaded. "Stand it down. Stand the whole thing down. For the love of your family, cease contact with these people."

Apparently, we couldn't take chances. This might well be a life-threatening situation. And on this last point, Kari took time to elaborate.

Daniel Pearl. Of the *Wall Street Journal.*

In 2002, Daniel was lured to a brutal death in Pakistan. The journalist had hoped for an interview that could shed light on Richard Reid, *the Shoe Bomber*, and his links with Al-Qaeda. His staunch desire for a breakthrough in his investigation may have clouded his judgment. Perhaps, it was pure bad luck.

As it turned out, the tragic case of Daniel Pearl was discussed at the table where Kari had sat with a bunch of higher-ups to assess the risks of my proposal. I had caused a mini-crisis, and my bosses were very anxious.

I would have been very flattered to know that all of this was to save me from myself. And strictly, as far as Kari Blackburn was concerned, it was. Clearly, she was fighting my corner. But then again, Kari revealed a detail too many that made me uneasy.

FORGET THE SAFETY and security concerns for a moment. At that table, the idea of the interview had initially generated excitement. The prospect of involvement in the biggest story to come out of Iraq since the fall of Baghdad seemed enticing.

However, the proposal quickly became "ludicrous" when a colleague, probably stuck in the sixties, realised that they would not be able to pursue the story if I were to be replaced by "a more orthodox voice of the BBC". Do you understand that?

When Kari said she was offended by the suggestion to replace me, I had no doubt that she was being sincere. This woman, who once stayed among African kids in Tanzania teaching them English, would not have found it funny that some outdated *suit-and-tie* would propose to replace me with a *more orthodox BBC voice* in order to satisfy his own prejudice.

Of course, Kari must have been offended.

For once, though, I was mad at the Boss over a detail. I was cross at her for sticking to her guns in her refusal to disclose the identity of the person who blasphemed against me.

"My dear, confidentiality is important," Kari had reasoned wisely, as she invited me to be the bigger person. As she argued, it is better to rise above negative opinions about you than to confront everyone who says something disparaging.

"Let's be grown-ups about this," the Boss added. "It is not helpful to know the names of your secret doubters. It is empowering to keep your mind free from such negative thoughts. I know that you understand."

Kari made sense.

Unfortunately, those thoughts were already there. I knew who the insensitive straight talker was at that table. The BBC, and Bush House as a whole, was a small world.

Kari concluded the *veto session* by repeating, "Before you go on with your day, disengage with your contacts. There will be no interview with Saddam Hussein. But this doesn't diminish the good work you've done out there."

These were words that dowsed the stubborn ambers of my fiery frustration; words that brought a balmy dose of solace.

But the ultimate solace would come much later from *within*, when—reflecting on my time in Iraq—my mind transported me back to Hillah, to the sight of the heaps of human remains, evidence of the monster's inhumanity.

How would I have remained neutral, sitting with the fugitive under cover of darkness somewhere near Tikrit, playing the devil's advocate, trying indecently to be impartial? How?

No, as you will see, Hillah doesn't allow for moral relativism. However you may look at it.

Chapter 26

THE MASS GRAVES OF HILLAH

This cloudless morning of May, in the company of most of Team BBC, I was back into my *North Face* jacket and trousers, with my gas mask buried in my kit, just in case. I couldn't see the poetry in this hanging sea of blue that would have filled me with a sense of peace and tranquillity, had this been in a serene corner of modern-day Kigali or somewhere in the mountains between Zurich and Davos. Understandably, the atmosphere in the convoy, with its indispensable security escort, was enough to spoil any view. But the real problem lay elsewhere. Worse than the cramped conditions in this convoy under heavy security, worse than the heat and the thirst, was my knowledge that the destination of our trip southward was a mass grave. The mass grave of Al-Mahawil.

A GROUP OF people, including men, women, and children, standing close in a circle, reminiscent of the communal Muslim prayer, as you would witness it out in the park on the last day of Ramadan. But instead of hearts singing out of divine grace, there are the heavy sounds of sniffles in the air. There's no bowing in pious prostration to Allah.

The only knees down against the soil are those of ordinary residents from the area and its surrounding. They are no forensic experts—they have never been anything of the sort. But with backhoes and bare hands, they dig, and sift in the ground.

The paydirt, of course, is no gold.

What the amateur hands bring to surface are fragments of what had once been human beings. Living, breathing human beings. Al-Mahawil, theatre of a macabre exercise in bone collection. And the yield is heaps of ribs, broken bones of decomposed limbs, skulls. And this yield is assorted in open display for bereaved families to inspect.

How many were they to have been piled together and interred here?

There's no agreement on a number. They have dug out remains of at least 3,000 and counting.

In this sombre setting—evidence of a vast and merciless tragedy—it's irrelevant whether George Bush and Tony Blair have lied about there being weapons of mass destruction. Here, it is outright indecent to wonder whether any reason, whatever it is, was good enough for the removal of Saddam Hussein.

HOW HAD IT all come to light? Well, it was a slow start. One news agency filed a *snap* into its wire system, which flashed up across computer terminals at the BBC. As per the highlights of the editorial memo I received from London, the first mass grave was discovered south of Hillah, around the time George Bush declared "Mission Accomplished." Then, two larger ones were uncovered a few days later—respectively near the village of al-Mahawil, north of Hillah, and in an open field in an agricultural area. Hillah turned overnight into an *epicentre of the macabre*, and London wanted reporters on the ground. And without the checkpoints, it would have taken us just a short drive.

The city, at some 100 kilometres from Baghdad, is located on the Euphrates River near ancient Babylon. In fact, it is the second largest city of one administrative division, the Babil Province, named after Babylon.

Hillah is home to the Imam Hussein Shrine; it's the burial place of Hussein ibn Ali, the grandson of Prophet Muhammad. In other words, Hillah is a holiest site for Shia Muslims, sworn adversaries of the Baath Administration, Saddam's Sunni-led regime. And the backstory of how the city had come to incur the vengeful wrath of Saddam is today a matter of popular record: In March 1991, in the wake of the first Gulf War, a group of Shiite demonstrators took to the streets of Hillah for a protest. It quickly turned into a brutal crackdown. After his defeat in Kuwait, Saddam had seized on the uprising to take out his pent-up frustration on the protesters. In a sheer display of violence, tanks and artillery of the Iraqi Army were deployed to shell the city; soldiers unleashed themselves into a door-to-door frenzy of killings and arrests.

These mass graves of Hillah, brought to light in the aftermath of the initial phase of the invasion, were the tragic, forgotten story of the thousands of those Shiite protesters who never made it back home, following that spring day of bloodshed.

IN HIS CALM voice, Omar Jumbe said, "You have 10 minutes for the two-way." He was speaking from a studio at the Centre Block of Bush House in London.

Omar —from *BBC Swahili*, as you may remember— headed a queue of programme hosts who awaited their turns for a pre-recorded two-way.

His voice rang very clear, but it was slightly altered by the satellite technology.

"Ten minutes?" I asked, sceptically. "What do I have to say to fill 10 minutes?

Omar never had a chance to reply; Studio Manager Neil Watson, looking sideway at me as though I had said something crazy, protested.

"I think 10 minutes will do us no justice," he said. "The whole programme—if it were up to me—should be you talking straight about this horrific find."

Neil had set me up safely at a few feet away from the busy excavation site. Facing the site, with two security details nearby, I looked back at the sound engineer who had propped himself up on a black hardcase, the better to stabilise his backside as he manned the transmission box.

Neil had a point. I hit the talkback button and opened the line again through to Omar who waited patiently.

"Make it 20 minutes," I suggested. "Neil thinks we have enough for the whole show. You want to change plans?"

"No," Omar said firmly. "It's 10 minutes max."

"Why?" I asked. "Think about it, at least."

"Venuste, that's not necessary," Omar said. "We have clips in the system, from *Human Rights Watch*. The Newsroom has provided transcripts for dubbing. We'll play these clips in the back of your two-way. So, focus on giving us the straight facts. Don't mention any comments from the same rights group we have here."

Clearly, Omar had things under control.

"You win, brother," I told him. "Shall we get started?"

The reply which came back was a countdown from five. Thereafter, down the satellite link, I could hear Omar going over his *lead*, rattling out the basic facts about Hillah, this epicentre of horror.

At last, he said, "Venuste Nshimiyimana, you are one of the *few* journalists who travelled to Hillah, 60 miles south of Baghdad. Can you give us a sense of what we are talking about?"

My mind went blank

Momentarily.

But the mental fog seemed to have lasted for the whole day, as my heart racked in my chest, *channelling* my fear that I might not find the right words in time. Somehow, I knew all would be fine.

When the microphone was live, and you were supposed to be speaking, the only way forward was to find the words, to make the story come alive. And that's what happened.

In fact, after I got over my anxious start, words flowed out of me.

Omar, swinging one question after another my way, ultimately said, "Before I let you go, Venuste, could you tell me how much of this horror, there at Hillah, relates to events and their aftermath in Rwanda back in 1994?"

Damn it, Omar!

Frustrated in his desire to bring up Rwanda when I first got to town, he had just decided to go for another try. And as his question ended, and as I tried to quickly process and deliver on his query, a bank of chaotic pictures rose up in a tangle across my mind. A mess.

Rwanda 1994?

This is the particular point of the timeline where

Omar's simple question had transported me: A return home, almost a decade after that exfiltration away into an uncertain sky. I had travelled through beautiful nature, all the way to this place that held fond memories of my childhood. In the flush countryside, I had stood atop *Mount Ibisi*, gazing in oppressive contemplation at the distant hills and valleys.

What had greeted me from below was literally the silence of the dead: My native hamlet of Gishamvu had gone quiet; the sound of hammers clanging on anvils had long since faded; no sound from any busy mills; and the neighbouring village of Sheke—which I would visit on the saddle of my bicycle—was just as deserted and quiet.

Painful homecoming.

From the top of *Mount Ibisi*, I had agonised over the impossible reunion with kith and kin. They were now imperceptible wisps of former lives. They now existed only in my mind. What had survived of them, and which seemed eternal to me, etched in the empty air, immune to erasure, was a string of names: Ndekwe, my father; Kanyanza, my brother; Shamagira, my sister, and then some more. Yes, some many more names: Lambert, Alexis, Rugamba, Concessa—an endless list, as it seemed. And here's the short of it: The hills and valleys opposite *Mount Ibisi* were now the silent abode of ghosts.

Today—these many years later—when these ghosts sprung to life in the empty theatre of my head, their silence became as loud as some accursed wailings from hell.

I mean, the Rwanda of 1994 is a realm of demons.

Demons that are mine as well as an entire nation.

I am now safe from them most of the time. But never when something came along to awaken them. And here, Omar had tripped a wire.

I quickly lost my composure. I now felt a tug at my heart. And when tears hit the back of my eyelids and a wail escaped my chest, Omar understood what he had done. He would spend the last seconds of the two-way as an improvised counsellor. Omar did nothing wrong.

Without intending it, he had exposed my trick for surviving Hillah—in fact, for surviving Baghdad.

See, these haunting memories from yesterday and my thoughts and feelings about the unfolding Iraqi tragedy; I kept them in separate *psychic* compartments. It was a necessary discipline. It kept me emotionally sober for the sake of the work at hand.

Omar had no way of knowing.

Chapter 27

A TOKEN OF FRIENDSHIP

It was 4:00 a.m. sharp when American private security contractors screened us through checkpoints and gates, directing us all the way into an indoor car park. Leaving Scheherazade there mounting vigil from the driver's seat of her cruiser, *Iman* and I worked our way onward. And progress was slow. We were held up here and there, as over-cautious agents announced us over their radio network. It would take us at least another quarter of an hour before we emerged face to face with the *de facto* American Governor of this fallen country.

PAUL BREMER MUST have preferred to *foreshadow* his crucial announcement on Al-Jazeera, rather than BBC Arabic. The Doha-based channel—a spin-off of one major BBC strategic venture that had gone south—had emerged as a unique binding phenomenon for some 300 million Arabs. The little trouble, however, was that these very Arabs were unhappy, in their majority, with the track-record of American foreign-policy interventions in their region.

While Al-Jazeera made sure they kept a finger on the pulse of global affairs, it also took upon itself to mirror their grievances back to them, in a way that was unfiltered. And that couldn't be a great proposition for politicians in Washington, or for Paul Bremer, by extension. From 9/11 to this invasion through the military campaign in Afghanistan, it had become undeniable that Washington had an *Al-Jazeera* problem. And it didn't help that an American fighter jet had recently killed the network's correspondent in the bombing of its Baghdad Bureau. In a nutshell, the parallel undeclared war between Al-Jazeera and the American troops was no fiction. Paul Bremer would be foolish to think that just handing them a scoop would be enough to warrant a cease-fire.

What then?

Bremer's office turned to a more traditional alternative. Since 1938, *BBC Arabic* had been a dependable platform for anyone with a message for the masses in the Arab world. Through wars and peacetimes, it had remained trusted and respected. And the good news was that the Americans had no outstanding grievances with BBC Arabic. As it happened, the scoop Bremer's office could have offered Al-Jazeera ended up in the inbox of *Iman*—*Iman* was part of *Team BBC* in Baghdad.

The memo had been stern. Just an invitation to a predawn brief with Paul Bremer at the presidential Palace in the Green zone. The bare details, however, were enough to pique the interest of any scoop-chasing journalist. After all, PR operatives knew well that there was nothing as effective as generating a curiosity gap, when reaching out to a media contact. This was especially true if you wanted them to show up at your door without much notice. What serious journalist, in their right mind, could resist a mysterious invitation to a predawn meeting with the *de facto* ruler of this fallen country?

Iman, a team player, had shared the memo with everyone. Now, what could the American official have to share that could warrant an early start? Was the potential story compelling enough to justify the trouble of defying the curfew?

The curfew wasn't lifted until 6:00 a.m.

For me, all these questions were irrelevant. After the episode of the great interview that never was, I was feeling a bit down. I prayed for an ultimate story that would be good enough to send me home on a triumphant note. This mysterious invitation to Saddam's old quarters was lofty with promise. I had to go.

But the rest of *Team BBC* just decided that nothing Paul Bremer had to say could take precedence over their need to extend their sleep through the dawn hours. In the end, we were a meagre trio to take the dawn trip to the Palace. There were two Arab ladies— *Imam* and the ever-present *Scheherazade,* who was back in her role as the driver. And there was one African—and that was me.

I INEXPLICABLY EXPECTED to be conflicted around the representative of George Bush, the single person who could have spared the world this war. But I guess I must have been distracted by how tall and how affable the *Governor* was. Unlike his security details who stood mean-faced in the wings, Bremer smiled charmingly as he shook hands with Iman and me.

"BBC Arabic, right?" he checked.

In fact, it was BBC Arabic and—through me—four other BBC services. The details would have been boring to Bremer, who probably hadn't slept the whole night. I chose to leave it to Iman to acquiesce at the banter.

His height, smile, and handshake. Later in the day—a lot more favourably than now—I would reassess the height, the smile, and the handshake of our affable host, when Bush House revelled in our scoop. Furthermore, our absent colleagues paid us full courtesy, crediting us across the vast BBC network for the exclusive Bremer soundbites. From an editorial perspective, Bremer was a saviour.

Later in the day, to compensate for our trouble at dawn, we didn't return to the Palace when in the afternoon, before a large media crowd, Bremer released details of *Order Number 2* of the Coalition Provisional Authority; the order that disbanded the Iraqi military, as well as the security and intelligence apparatus of Saddam Hussein.

CUPPING THE BOOK in both hands, delaying whatever she intended to do with it, Scheherazade spoke almost regretfully.

"I am not sure if I will ever see you when you are gone tomorrow," she said. "But if I live, it will be hard for me to forget you." She chuckled sadly. "You are quite the unicorn."

The landlady had been aloof since that dawn encounter with Bremer.

She had been demolished by the content of the scoop and had found her feelings at odd with our excitement, which was purely on professional grounds. Iman and I were not in jubilation; we were over the moon for being handed an exclusive on a platter. But that had not been obvious to the landlady.

On that return drive from the Palace, as we were lost in the fever of dressing up the story for broadcast, we unwittingly exuded all the wrong kind of vibes—We were eager like a carrion crow on the cusp of a feast. And that was not going down well with my *super fixer*.

Apparently, disbanding the Iraqi army was supposed to be a second *naqba*. The Americans who had supposedly come with freedom in their *Abrams* tanks had just taken the last step towards a full "colonisation" of Iraq, the cradle of the Islamic Golden Age. Why were Iman and I not outraged? Why the hell were we so excited?

Scheherazade had it wrong. Journalists are just hard to understand sometimes. An earthquake or a tsunami would get us all excited. But would it be out of fun? Hell, no.

To be honest, I am not even sure if I can ever accurately convey the type of feeling that seizes us when we have our hands on a compelling story. But let's say it's closer to the agitation of folly rather than the serene bliss of fun.

Scheherazade needed the time it took. But she now understood. After more than a week of aloofness—and now realising that we only had this one last evening in Baghdad—she had walked into the familiar tearoom with more than dinner. She had brought along a token. And was now giving a speech that had the air of a farewell address.

"If you live?" I asked, musing on what she had just said, unable to take my eyes off the book, a paperback that was intriguing, if only by the plainness of its cover. "What do you mean by that?"

The landlady looked down aimlessly at the book. "I have placed myself in your power," she stated. "I carefully did. Because there's something in you that's inviting of trust. I let it guide me like a morning star. Then, the interview never happened. Which is a shame. But am I all clear of a nasty surprise?" That was too enigmatic.

"You speak in parables," I said. "This can mean just about anything. What's going on?"

Her hands played on the book. "Money is a powerful motivator," she declared. "What do you think would happen if someone finds out about me?"

I would not have understood her if I didn't have the whole context of our dealings over the last month.

"Why did you think it was safe to make that offer of interview to me, in the first place? It's not really because I am from Africa. Is it?"

Scheherazade responded as though she had rehearsed her answer.

"Not really," she said. "But if you were some *white boy*, I would certainly never have taken the risk."

I glanced at her.

She looked very sad.

Without a prompt on my part, she continued: "Here's why I really felt confident enough to place myself in your power: You talk a lot about your daughters; you pray to God before you go to bed, before you start the day. You believe in Heaven and Hell. Then, there's your personal story. The Genocide. The suffering your people went through. If you can't be trusted, there is no hope in mankind."

I took this in, wondering how much exactly I had been going on about my daughters, about the *Lord's prayer*, and about Rwanda. Then I remembered

Scheherazade had regularly made enquiries about my family, wondering whether all was fine back home. I didn't know the way I spoke of the girls would carry a particular meaning to whoever would be listening.

"What's changed, then?" I asked. "Am I suddenly different on my last evening in Baghdad?"

"Nothing has changed," the woman said. "Perhaps, I just need to have this conversation."

"Good," I said. "But do you know I never mentioned you, by any reference, even to my bosses in London? They knew not to push for a disclosure."

She stared sadly at me. "Really?"

"You have to understand this," I said: "The anonymous source of a journalist is sacred. And Journalism will die when we all become dishonourable men who couldn't care about our own ethics. Trust me, I will abandon this line of work before I ever bring dishonour upon myself."

The silence that fell between us was only broken when Scheherazade stood off and offered to hug me—an unprecedented move.

I awkwardly indulged her.

Then, she took my hand, turned my palm up, and placed the book in it.

"It's my personal copy," she said. "A token of my friendship."

With the book now in my possession, I could read its title—*Zabiba and the King*. The author was not identified.

"You wrote this?" I asked.

She smiled. "No, I did not."

"Who's the author, then?"

"President Saddam," she smiled faintly. "And down there is his signature. He had personally dedicated it to me in that Palace the Americans have now defiled."

The faint smile of the woman briefly became a sad scoff. Now, I could see that her lips were slightly parched. Now, her sadness wore no veil.

Zabiba and the King. I was shocked.

My lingering doubt evaporated—my doubt that Shahida belonged to that circle of Baath members who had gone underground, now forced to disguise their loyalty in the new chaotic Baghdad under American boots.

I looked at the book again.

I thought of something to say—anything at all. But nothing that made sense came. So, I offered Scheherazade a hug of commiseration.

When we let go, she spoke and there was a resurgent hope in her voice.

"He is safe," she said. "President Saddam is safe, and he is not giving up. He has more of his people behind him than the Americans would like the world to think." There was a pause.

Then, one last time, Shahida the Enigma, my super fixer, my *Scheherazade* said, "Saddam will return. He is safe."

THREE YEARS LATER, I sat before my TV set in London, repressing tears as I remembered that empty ring of optimism in Scheherazade's voice. She had been wrong in her reading of the future. There would be no return of Saddam. Ever. And the news on television was clear about it.

As it happened, shortly before the Muslim prayer of *Eid al-Adha*, the life story of Saddam Hussein came to an end with a hangman slipping a noose around his neck, snapping it on camera. I wondered whether Scheherazade was watching the news.

Chapter 28

IT'S TRUE WHAT THEY SAY

For the homeward trip to London, we had to retrace our steps via Kuwait and Jordan. The inbound journey was just as punishing as the outbound one. It was as equally fraught with danger as it was lengthy. It included that eight-hours' drive from Baghdad to the Kuwaiti border. Halfway through, we stopped for lunch. And lunch was nothing fancy.

All we had for it was the meagre rations of corned beef supplied by the Coalition soldiers we had left behind. The corned beef was good, for sure. But taste was none of our worries. Anything edible at this point would have been just delicious. No, our concern was that there wasn't enough of the beef brisket for everyone. Sure, we had kept up our collective impulse to share, but that was of no practical use now. For sharing to work, one needs to have enough of what that is to be shared. As it happened, we were in a little pickle.

Briefly considering the situation, an awareness dawned upon me.

This is it, I told myself. *Here's where we settle this matter.*

But what was the matter?

BACK AT THE start in Amman, our team had bonded quickly, despite hardly knowing each other. Our shared mission and perilous journey melted away boundaries of class, race, gender, and pay grade. We instantly became more than colleagues. We became friends.

To minimise the risk of editorial blunders, we worked together and sought advice from each other, holding on carefully to our roadmap. Whenever possible, we had lunches and suppers together. In that villa, we bunked in pairs like soldiers in the barracks. Overall, in this city of shortages, we had to be selfless. Like hell, we had to *really* care for each other.

Stephen Sackur and I shared a second-floor ensuite with separate compartments. We took turns showering and shaving in front of the large mirror. I was one of the occasional odd cooks around, and I got *cheers* for my salad and meat recipes. On weekends, Team BBC gathered to eat dishes Scheherazade personally delivered from her home kitchen.

These collective dinners were more than just about the food. They were moments that reminded us of our common, fragile humanity at a time and in a place where death had become a trivial matter.

Especially, these evenings we spent together reminded me of some lost childhood memories. In the Africa I grew up, one rarely belonged to themselves—one was always part of *the group*. And to share was perceived as a reliable indication that a person's heart was in the right place.

Throughout our stay, Stephen Sackur insisted on giving the youngest member of Team BBC more attention, like a big brother. When there were only three bottles of water or one packet of biscuits to share, he would turn to me.

"Here you go, Venuste," Stephen would offer avuncularly, but with humour and forcefully. "You have it! You're the youngest."

Always with a knowing grin, I would carefully remind the team that looks might indeed be very deceptive. With a smiling heart, I would argue that it wouldn't be the first time in history if your designated youngest one turned out to be a lot older. But the team wanted no questions asked.

As far as they were concerned, the question was settled—I was the youngest. The only outstanding matter of importance was to ensure that the *youngest* was well looked after.

However, one other member of the team was willing

to listen to my playful protests. That was *Eon*, our BBC Scotland colleague.

"Guys," *Eon* would plead, arguing rather carefully, aware that the subject was a tad risky. "Guys, there's something to be taken seriously about the case, which is often made, that *blacks don't crack*."

"And what's your ingenious theory here, Eon," Barbara Plett challenged, a subtle way of telling Eon to tread carefully—very carefully.

"Well," Eon said, "I wouldn't volunteer to accurately guess the age of a black person. And I say this rather enviously. Beyond their teens, the aging process seems to slow down for black people. If you ask me, Venuste might well be our eldest. In fact, I am sure of it. And I am warning you!"

Eon stood no chance.

They barely registered his considered opinion and never believed a word of what he had to say.

That was all the better as far as I could say. But I knew I ultimately had to find a way to vindicate Eon. And one incident almost pre-empted what I intended to leave until the end.

On our expedition to Hillah, temperatures were at their peak. The Mercury hovered around 45 degrees Celsius. Oh God, it was extremely hot—Even for me, the African.

Under this sweltering heat, our water supply dwindled down to the very last bottle. The situation was testing to the human character. And then, Stephen

Sackur proved he was serious about his commitment to look after the youngest.

Upon taking stock of our sorry state of affairs, Stephen—now under the acute spur of thirst—realised he would violate his own dispositions if he went for the remaining bottle. And when he reached for it, it was only to offer it to me.

Of course, I wanted the last bottle of water. In this scorching heat, who wouldn't? But I couldn't abuse Stephen Sackur's generosity. I had to pretend I wasn't thirsty.

So, I argued it wasn't fair for me to drink up the bottle, simply because I was the youngest, while someone else actually needed it more.

"You might be the eldest, Stephen," I said, "But you are the one with the parched lips here. You could do a lot with this bloody bottle."

Though he was clearly thirsty, Stephen reluctantly accepted the water. Right there, for the first time on this return trip of ours from Hillah, I considered ending the running gag. I had signed up to it for the harmless fun, but this wasn't fun anymore.

However, I decided to wait for a better opportunity to vindicate Eon. That opportunity didn't show until our lunch stopover, halfway on our journey back towards Kuwait City.

SO, IN THIS stretch of desert sand—still on the Iraqi side of the border—we were a bunch of us. But not enough beef brisket to go around. I was done with the game. The fun had run its course.

It ends here, I told myself.

Without fanfare, I sprang my cheeky trick on the team. "If everyone agrees," I suggested loudly, "the youngest of us should get the last of the beef."

As far as they were concerned, I was the youngest And with that certainty on their mind, they looked at me, somewhat puzzled. They had given me a privilege, and now, apparently, I wanted to abuse it. But did they really know what I was up to?

I said, "If you don't object, let's find out."

"Find out what?" Stephen asked.

"We don't know for sure who the youngest is," I said with a grin. "But there's only one way to find out." The eyes were still on me as I continued, "Your ID cards! Your passports! Let's take the guesswork out of this."

The puzzlement faded from the faces. The team, now on the same page as me, found my suggestion fun. Within a minute, they produced their documents. I took a few seconds to examine the passports, then proclaimed the result. The colleagues took turns to double-check.

"Guys," Eon hollered first, feeling vindicated. "I told you. You cannot accurately read the age of black people by appearance alone."

"Venuste," Stephen called. He looked seriously bemused at my bout of merriment . "You can't possibly be the oldest of our lot?"

"Not me," I said, all in stitches. "Your grievance, should you have one, is with the documents."

According to the passports , I was born on a 12ᵗʰ January, and Stephen Sackur had turned up on God's Green Footstool a full year later on a 9ᵗʰ January.

In other words, I had been breathing for more than twelve months when the future great interviewer sucked in his first lungful of air. And here's the bottomline: No one was older than me in this team, here in the Arabian desert, on its way home from Baghdad.

"I told you," Eon shouted once more, pointing a triumphant finger at Barbara Plett. "Blacks don't *fucking* crack."

I turned to Eon, with a wide smile and a thumbs-up. "Yes, my white brother! You are damn right."

Eon nodded fantastically, looking very pleased. And as it were, Eon—our colleague from BBC Scotland— had been the youngest all the way.

WELCOME BACK

Poised before the large studio console, Studio Manager Jeff Brown listened intently as the *Greenwich pips* ticked away. The repeating burst of the sharp signal piped out in sync with the progress of the dotted red light on the wall. It was a feature of precision that added a layer of drama to the countdown ritual under way.

At the top of the hour, with a flick of his finger, Jeff flooded the studio with the iconic drumbeat sound—the programme's opening signature.

Listening to the enthralling rhythm, I marvelled at the knowledge that, exactly at the very moment, across cities on the Continent—Accra, Lagos, Abuja, Abidjan, Freetown, Ouagadougou, Kigali, Monrovia, Nairobi—across these cities all over the Continent, the upbeat festival of drums beamed simultaneously into the sets of millions of listeners.

I had met countless BBC enthusiasts on my trips, and was always transfixed by their harmless zeal. The thought of them listening religiously to the BBC rarely failed to remind me that I should never give anything short of my best to this broadcasting business. Any work half done was a betrayal of their trust.

Ten seconds into the news hour, the drumrolls in the studio turned into a dry wailing of flutes. Jeff Brown, still fully alert, slammed a foot into a pedal beneath the mixers' table. A red light flashed in front of the presenter who sat beyond the dividing wall of glass. And as Jeff progressively dipped the music bed down to half its full decibels, a familiar voice came across through the subwoofers.

"It's 15:00 GMT," the voice proclaimed. "You are listening to the BBC, and this is *Focus on Africa* with me, Hassan Arouni." The drumbeat peaked up briefly, then dipped again, and the show steamed ahead.

Meanwhile, in this outer compartment of the studio, we were all quiet as Jeff Brown dextrously manoeuvred Hassan through the headline segment, alternating between shouting *CUE* and *CLIP* into the presenter's headphones. It was 60 seconds of ultimate focus, 60 seconds of tension.

The tension subsided during the ensuing session of the news bulletin, read from another studio. But this recess in the drama was temporary. The bulletin—sanctified core stuff from the BBC's Central Newsroom—lasted just five short minutes. It wasn't long before the red light flashed on again in front of Hassan, prompting him to cue up a pre-recorded dispatch.

As trailed in the headlines, it was a heart-rending account of the latest update on the flare-up of violence in Baghdad—a dispatch from the BBC's Caroline Hawley.

As the tape started to unfold, Jeff punched a finger into the talkback button and informed the presenter, "Two minutes, 30 seconds on tape!"

These constant reminders, though redundant, were useful to keep the presenter focused. And the next time Jeff provided an update on the tape's progress, he turned to me and gently admonished, "Are you still gonna do this?"

Startled, I said, "What?"

Without looking my way, the studio manager advised, "You better be sitting in there now. You're up next."

Of course, I thought.

Anxious excitement fluttered in the pit of my stomach as I lurched forward and leaned hard against the heavy slab of the soundproof door, cranking it open to enter the presenter's side of the studio. I quickly took my seat opposite the presenter, with my back to the glass wall through which they waved to the studio operator. After the indispensable level check, I took a deep breath and was good to go.

"45 seconds on tape," Jeff barked again into our

headphones. And 45 seconds later, in the back of the pre-recorded dispatch, Hassan Arouni was saying, "With me now in the studio is the BBC's Venuste Nshimiyimana who just returned from Baghdad. Venuste, welcome back!"

FOR A BBC studio two-way, this one was exceptionally long. The most generous output producer would not have allocated more than five minutes for this kind of banter, but Hassan Arouni had kept the questions coming, well past the seven-minute mark. Perhaps it was all in the spirit of making the most of the money the BBC had spent on my duty trip. At any rate, *value for money* was a watchword around Bush House.

So, the questions kept coming: Are the Coalition troops really in control of Baghdad, from what you could assess first-hand? With everything that's going on, do residents share the optimism of George Bush who declared "Mission Accomplished" about a month ago? How are the Coalition forces going about locating Saddam's weapons of mass destruction? Is the Coalition transparent about casualties among its own ranks?

All the questions—unlike those we would put to outside guests who had their own self-serving agendas—had been agreed on with me. Interviews with the BBC's own correspondents were grounded on what the correspondents knew for sure.

It's said that a good barrister never puts a question

to a witness at the stand without a foreknowledge of what the answer is likely to be. Like the barrister, the presenter—for different reasons—wouldn't put a question to a colleague with no knowledge of the answer. It was highly against orthodoxy to do such a thing. In extreme cases, it could lead to grievances and the collapse of working relationships.

My point here is that I had solid answers to all of Hassan's questions, except for his last one.

To wrap up the studio two-way, the presenter said, "A reminder that, live here with me in the *Focus on Africa* studio, is the BBC's Venuste Nshimiyimana. Before I let you go, how was it personally for you, reporting from Baghdad? Baghdad was a long way from home, wasn't it?"

The question was *code*, and nothing malicious was intended. Hassan Arouni, a consummate professional, knew no malice. No, Hassan was legitimately probing for something personal. If he were to be blunt, he would have said, "Was it harder for you reporting in Iraq as a black person?"

Hassan knew that bluntness could have come across as offensive, especially to his millions of listeners who might infer *race-baiting*. That's why he phrased his question subtly. But was it *race-baiting* anyway?

No, that would have been beneath the veteran presenter and the professional team behind the show. They knew that black staff members who report on global events often face the added stress of *being black*.

Even as part of the same BBC team, we often ended up dealing with inappropriate scrutiny, as we headed—right behind untroubled white colleagues—to a site of an event, or even past ID control.

As a stoic person, I am utterly disgusted at ever playing the race card. But quite beyond our control, the race card would occasionally be played on us. And when it happens, we would carefully keep it under wraps, and the audience tuning in would suspect nothing. But occasionally, it was insightful to lift the veil on the unspoken *backstories* of our *lead stories*.

Again, Presenter Arouni wasn't *race-baiting*.

As he said it, *Baghdad was a long way from home.* And black journalists weren't a dime a dozen in the city. The other black correspondent there, whom I remember, was the formidable Rageh Omar. Now, was my assignment more of a burden because I was black?

Quite the contrary.

Being African in Baghdad was endearing to the Iraqis I interviewed. I felt that they engaged me sincerely, without suspicion. The enigmatic Scheherazade—in her own shocking admission—would not have offered me the interview that never was if I were white. And overall, I felt less at risk of being kidnapped by an angry Saddam loyalist. Iraqis had no reason to believe that Africans were behind their nightmare.

Ironically, it was back at Bush House that some fellow had the idea that I wasn't enough of an "orthodox BBC voice" to conduct a high-profile interview. Apart from that blip, being black in Baghdad made my assignment easier and safer.

So, how did I respond to Hassan Arouni, the presenter?

Well, I flashed him a smile, and asked rhetorically, "Was reporting in Baghdad harder for me than anybody else?"

"Yes, was it?" Hassan said.

I said with a chuckle, "That is one question I didn't have the luxury to ask."

Laughing, Hassan prodded genuinely, "How so?"

"With all the dangers in Baghdad," I said somewhat vaguely, "we needed all the focus we could muster, rather than engage in identity navel-gazing. And I can tell you, Hassan, that I was no more exposed to the danger of the war than any of my other BBC colleagues. I'd say I have never worked with nicer colleagues under harder circumstances."

AT HER DESK back on the *Focus On Africa* newsroom floor—safe from the open microphones in *Studio 33*—a woman who monitored the ongoing transmission said, "Bullshit."

The woman was BBC Africa's Senior Editor, Josephine Hazeley.

Josephine was an energetic force of nature, known for telling things as they were. She was alien to the subtle art of mincing her words.

Perhaps, Josephine was right.

SOURCES AND FURTHER READING

This book is a record of lived experience, primarily informed by the people I encountered, interviewed, bickered with, learned from, loved, and hated. They were my irreplaceable academy on the human condition.

Iraqis, Jordanians, Kuwaitis, British, Americans, French, Africans—young and old, despondent, and hopeful, colleagues (friendly and unpleasant), soldiers and civilians—all taught me something about life that's now part of me. They were my primary sources.

To ensure the integrity of historical accounts, I relied on my own contemporaneous observations as a reporter, and on contemporaneous reporting by the BBC and other reputable news organisations, including *The Guardian*, *Le Monde*, *The New York Times*,

The Atlantic, *The Independent*, *The Washington Post*, and *Time*.

I consulted reports of official inquiries, including parliamentary reports, and watched hours of relevant footage from the US *Army University Press*. The following bibliographical and online references also proved useful in widening my scope, refreshing my perspective, and ensuring the accuracy of historical facts.

GENERAL REFERENCES

Geoff Simons, *Iraq: From Sumer to Post-Saddam* (London: Palgrave Macmillan, 23 December 2003).

——*The Scourging of Iraq: Sanctions, Law and Natural Justice* (London: Springer, September 1996).

James Arnold, *Saddam Hussein's Iraq, 2nd Edition* (Lerner Publishing Group, 1 Aug 2012).

Thomas Ricks, *Fiasco: The American Military Adventure in Iraq* (New York: The Penguin Press, 2006).

Frédéric Bozo, *Histoire Secrète de la Crise Irakienne: La France, les Etats-Unis et l'Irak, 1991-2003* (Paris, Perrin, 2013).

Bob Woodward, *Plan Of Attack* (New York, London, Toronto, Sydney: Simon & Schuster, 2004).

Jehane Noujaim, *Control Room, A Documentary* (Noujaim Films & Magnolia Pictures, 2004).

John Simpson, *The Wars Against Saddam: Taking the Hard Road to Baghdad* (London: Pan, 2004).

Rageh Omaar, *Revolution Day: The Human Story of the Battle for Iraq* (London: Penguin, 2005).

Josh Rushing, *Mission Al-Jazeera: Build a Bridge, Seek the Truth, Change the World* (Palgrave MacMillan, 2007).

George Packer, *The Assassins' Gate: America in Iraq* (London: Faber & Faber Limited, 2006).

David Zucchino, *Thunder Run: The Armored Strike To Capture Baghdad* (New York: Atlantic Books, 2004).

George Galloway, *Mr Galloway Goes To Washington: The Brit Who Set Congress Straight About Iraq* (New York, London: The New Press, 2005).

Craig Whitlock , *The Afghanistan Papers: A Secret History of the War* (New York, London, Toronto: Simon & Schuster, 2021).

Council On Foreign Relations, *2003-2011: The Iraq War* (CFR, Retrieved on 03 October 2023: https://www.cfr.org/timeline/iraq-war).

Britannica.com, *Iraq War: 2003—2011* (The Britannica Group, Retrieved on 03 October 2023: https://www.britannica.com/event/Iraq-War).

BBC News, *The events that led to war in Iraq, Video* (London, 6 Jul 2016, Retrieved on 3 October 2023: https://youtu.be/6daSrkgDX-0k?si=ekEwcQRNEdSwt7jj).

Sir John Chilcot, *The Report of the Iraq Inquiry* (London: Crown copyright, 2016).

INTRODUCTION: WHEN NO ONE IS WATCHING

Bob Woodward, *Bush at War*, (Simon & Schuster Ltd, 2002)

Committee On Foreign Relations, U.S. Senate, *Tora Bora Revisited: How We Failed To Get Bin Laden And Why It Matters Today* (U.S. Government Printing Office, 2009).

Carter Malkasian, *The American War in Afghanistan: A History* (Oxford University press, 2021).

Venuste Nshimiyimana, *Prélude du Génocide Rwandais* (Louvain-la-Neuve, Editions Quorum, 1995).

Fergal Keane, *Season of Blood: A Rwandan Journey* (London: Penguin, 1996).

Roméo Dallaire, *Shake Hands With The Devil: The Failure of Humanity in Rwanda*, (Arrow, 2005).

Colette Braeckman, *Rwanda: Mille Collines, Mille Douleurs* (Éditions Nivicata:, 2014).

——*Rwanda: Histoire d'un génocide* (Fayard, 1994).

CH 1: NATION SHALL SPEAK UNTO NATION

Renée Dickason, *Genèse de la BBC ou les balbutiements de sa Majesté des ondes* (Revue Française de Civilisation Britannique, 05 December 2020, Retrieved on 04 October 2023: http://journals.openedition.org/rfcb/7433).

Bush House: The iconic home of BBC World Service (BBC, July 2019, Retrieved on 03 October 2023: https://www.bbc.com/historyofthebbc/buildings/bush-house/).

Dr Alban Webb, *Empire & Europe: How the BBC found a balance between Empire and Europe, English and foreign language broadcasting* (BBC, 11

July 2019, Retrieved on 03 October 2023: https://www.bbc.com/historyofthebbc/100-voices/people-nation-empire/empire-and-europe/).

——*Emigres: How Did The BBC Become A United Nations of broadcasting?* (BBC, 11 July 2019, Retrieved on 03 October 2023: https://www.bbc.com/historyofthebbc/100-voices/people-nation-empire/emigres/).

Houcine Msaddek, *BBC Arabic (1938-1995): Soft Power or Reithian Practice Abroad?* (Revue Française de Civilisation Britannique, 05 December 2020, Retrieved on 03 October 2023: http://journals.openedition.org/rfcb/7056).

British Library, *The Establishment of BBC Arabic & Egyptian 'Nahwy'* (London, 04 October 2017, Retrieved on 3 October 2023: https://blogs.bl.uk/asian-and-african/2017/10/the-establishment-of-bbc-arabic-egyptian-nahwy.html).

Trevor Harris, *John Reith and the BBC 1922-1939: Building an Empire of the Air?* (Revue Française de Civilisation Britannique, 05 December 2020, Retrieved on 03 October 2023: http://journals.openedition.org/rfcb/7498).

CH 4: THE ROAD TO BOOTCAMP

BBC News, *"This is just a scene from hell"*, BBC News, 6 April 2003, (Retrieved on 3 October 2023: http://news.bbc.co.uk/1/hi/world/middleeast/2921807.stm).

The Guardian, *Simpson recovering from 'friendly fire' attack* (The Guardian, 7 April 2003, Retrieved on 3 October 2023: https://www.theguardian.com/media/2003/apr/07/iraq.iraqandthemedia1).

CH 5: CAPTAIN DORIAN SMITH
Josh Rushing, *Mission Al-Jazeera: Build a Bridge, Seek the Truth, Change the World* (Palgrave MacMillan, 2007).
——*SPIN: The Art of Selling War, A Two-Part Documentary* (Al-Jazeera, 2004, Retrieved on 03 October 2023: https://www.youtube.com/watch?v=Sm4g7ujkiO0 ; https://www.youtube.com/watch?v=ulzhdxdj9cY).
Michael Hudson, *Washington vs. Al Jazeera: Competing Constructions of Middle East Realities* (Arab Media & Society, 1 March, 2005, Retrieved on 3 October 2023: https://www.arabmediasociety.com/washington-vs-al-jazeera-competing-constructions-of-middle-east-realities/)
Jehane Noujaim, *Control Room, A Documentary* (Noujaim Films & Magnolia Pictures, 2004, Trailer Retrieved on 03 October 2023: https://www.youtube.com/watch?v=T-C-pf6ZPmw).

CH 15: CLEOPATRA'S NOSE
Paul Saka, *Pascal's Wager about God* (Internet Encyclopedia of Philosophy, Retrieved on 04 October 2023: https://iep.utm.edu/pasc-wag/).

Marc Fourny, *Le nez de Cléopâtre a-t-il vraiment changé l'Histoire ?* (Le Point, 03 December 2022, Retrieved on 04 October 2023: https://www.lepoint.fr/histoire/le-nez-de-cleopatre-a-t-il-vraiment-change-l-histoire-03-12-2022-2500247_1615.php).

CH 16: THE HIGHWAY OF DEATH
Geoff Simons, *Iraq: From Sumer to Post-Saddam* (London: Palgrave Macmillan, 23 December 2003).

Robert Jensen, *The Gulf War Brought Out the Worst in Us* (Los Angeles Times, 22 May 2000, Retrieved on 04 October 2023: https://www.latimes.com/archives/la-xpm-2000-may-22-me-32819-story.html).

CH 19: BAGHDAD IS FALLING
David Zucchino, *Thunder Run: The Armored Strike To Capture Baghdad* (New York: Atlantic Books, 2004).s

Army University Press, *Operation Iraqi Freedom: The Drive to Baghdad, A Documentary* (Army University Press Films, 2020, Retrieved on 3 October 2023: https://www.youtube.com/watch?v=O7pbW1QoPaI)

——*Operation Iraqi Freedom: The Fight for Baghdad* (Army University Press Films, 2020, Retrieved on 03 October 2023: https://youtu.be/d8uaFZAxzp-w?si=JVTx4yIn8Pu7sF7O)

CH 19: THE KILLER ROUND

The Guardian, *Tank captain admits firing on media hotel*, 21 April 2003 (Retrieved on 3 October 2023: https://www.theguardian.com/world/2003/apr/21/usa.iraq1).

Joel Campagna and Rhonda Roumani, *Permission to Fire?* (New York: CPJ, 27 May 2003, Retrieved on 03 October 2023: https://cpj.org/reports/2003/05/palestine-hotel/).

CH 23: THE FRENCH CONNECTION

Le Monde, *Nous Sommes Tous Américains* (Paris, 12 September 2001, Retrieved on 03 October 2023: https://www.lemonde.fr/archives/article/2001/09/13/nous-sommes-tous-americains_4188452_1819218.html).

CNN, Chirac: France stands with U.S. vs. terrorism (CNN, 18 September 2001, Retrieved on 03 October 2023: https://edition.cnn.com/2001/US/09/18/ret.bush.chirac/index.html).

Dominique de Villepin, French address on Iraq at the UN Security Council (New York: 14 February 2003, Retrieved on 04 October 2023: https://en.wikisource.org/wiki/French_address_on_Iraq_at_the_UN_Security_Council ; Video: https://www.youtube.com/watch?v=2gpnXF5KRM4&t=18s).

Leah Pisar, *Orage sur l'Atlantique: La France, les Etats-Unis Face à l'Irak* (Paris: Fayard, 2010).

Frédéric Bozo, *Histoire secrète de la crise irakienne: La France, les Etats-Unis et l'Irak*, 1991-2003 (Paris, Perrin, 2013)

CH 26: THE MASS GRAVES OF HILLAH

James Arnold, *Saddam Hussein's Iraq, 2nd Edition* (Lerner Publishing Group, 1 Aug 2012).

CH 27: A TOKEN OF FRIENDSHIP

The Atlantic, *Donald Rumsfeld's Hate-Love-Hate Relationship with Al Jazeera*, 4 October 2011, (Retrieved on 3 October 2023: https://www.theatlantic.com/international/archive/2011/10/donald-rumsfelds-hate-love-hate-relationship-al-jazeera/337117/).

Michael Hudson, *Washington vs. Al Jazeera: Competing Constructions of Middle East Realities* (Arab Media & Society, 1 March, 2005, Retrieved on 3 October 2023: https://www.arabmediasociety.com/washington-vs-al-jazeera-competing-constructions-of-middle-east-realities/).

ACKNOWLEDGEMENT

The BBC's late Kari Blackburn did more than just believe in me. It was this formidable woman who picked me for my pivotal assignment to Baghdad. Kari valued my gift as a multilinguist who spoke four of the BBC World Service's broadcast languages. In her quite flattering words, I was her *four reporters rolled into one*. It's obvious that she gave me confidence I never knew I had. For that, Kari, I thank you.

On to my *clan*—my life as a broadcaster was demanding on my family. Dedeli, Astrida, and Isaro accommodated my lengthy absences from home, and my duty trip to Iraq carried the added stress that I might not have returned. Your patience and understanding were my fuel, family. I love you all.

Now, what else?

Candid Intent is about people in various places, from London to Baghdad. If you are one of those, regardless of whether you helped or hindered my journey; regardless of whether you were a hero or villain, I thank you for the experience of my encounter with you. There would have been nothing to write about without your kindness or your nasty dispositions.

And here, we arrive at a special *thank you*. And it goes to my editor, publisher, and fellow ex-BBC broadcaster, Lamine Konkobo *aka* Equiano d' Sassa. He was an absolute pain, but his relentless attention to detail was invaluable. He took full responsibility for refining and enhancing the manuscript, providing robust feedback, fact-checking it, and brutally editing it for clarity, concision and coherence.

Finally, to all the *anonymous* and *anonymised* ones who deserve a mention for their role in my story, I present my gratitude. To put it simply, you are all amazing.

INDEX